Behind the Lines

Creative Writing with Offenders and People at Risk

Michael Crowley

Behind the Lines
Creative Writing with Offenders and People at Risk
Michael Crowley

Published 2012 by
Waterside Press Ltd
Sherfield Gables
Sherfield on Loddon
Hook, Hampshire
United Kingdom RG27 0JG

Telephone +44(0)1256 882250
E-mail enquiries@watersidepress.co.uk
Online catalogue WatersidePress.co.uk

ISBN 978-1-904380-78-8 (Paperback)   **ISBN** 978-908162-12-0 (e-book)

Cataloguing-In-Publication Data A catalogue record for this book can be obtained on request from the British Library.

Cover design © 2012 Waterside Press. Design by www.gibgob.com.

UK distributor Gardners Books, 1 Whittle Drive, Eastbourne, East Sussex, BN23 6QH. Tel: +44 (0)1323 521777; sales@gardners.com; www.gardners.com

North American distributor International Specialized Book Services (ISBS), 920 NE 58th Ave, Suite 300, Portland, Oregon, 97213, USA. Tel: 1 800 944 6190 Fax: 1 503 280 8832; orders@isbs.com; www.isbs.com

Printed by MPG-Biddles Ltd, Kings Lynn.

e-book *Behind the Lines: Creative Writing with Offenders and People at Risk* is available as an ebook and also to subscribers of Myilibrary and Dawsonera (for ISBN see above).

Behind the Lines

Creative Writing with Offenders and People at Risk

Michael Crowley

With a Foreword by David Ramsbotham

 **WATERSIDE** PRESS

CONTENTS

5   Past and Future Scenes   153

6   What Poetry Can Do · 199

7   Action into Words · 223

By the same author:

The Man They Couldn't Hang

A Tale of Murder, Mystery and Celebrity

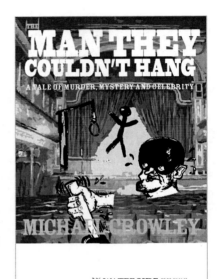

A play in two Acts with an Introduction by the author.

The story of John 'Babbacombe' Lee is one of the most bizarre in English criminal history. Lee is the only person to have been reprieved by a Home Secretary after standing on a gallows trap which failed to open. This happened at Exeter Prison in 1885 when the notoriously inept public hangman James Berry gave up after three failed attempts. Lee spent 22 years in prison before being released.

> **❝ This work would undoubtedly provide a wealth of meaty material for any drama workshop worth its name, whether inside or outside of the prison wall. I hope to have the opportunity to see it performed some time, if only to have a good laugh at a good (or rather bad) hanging ❞**
>
> *Prison Service Journal*

Paperback ISBN 978-1-904380-64-1 | Ebook ISBN 978-1-906534-97-4

140 pages | Sept 2010

Full details **WatersidePress.co.uk/hang**

THE AUTHOR

Michael Crowley is a youth justice worker and writer. His stage plays include 'Beyond Omarska', 'The Man They Couldn't Hang' (Waterside Press 2010) 'A Warning Against Idle Gossip' and 'The Cell' (24/7 Theatre Festival Manchester 2012). 'Close to Home', a collection of poetry, is published by Prolebooks this year.

He has written for youth theatre and been writer in residence at a young offender institution for the past five years. He lives in West Yorkshire. See also www.michaelcrowley.co.uk

AUTHOR OF THE FOREWORD

Lord David Ramsbotham GCB, CBE was a a British Army general before serving as Her Majesty's Chief Inspector of Prisons from 1995 to 2001. During that time he became well-known for his attempts to improve prison conditions, encourage rehabilitation strategies and his preparedness to challenge the authorities. In 2005 he was elevated to the House of Lords as Baron Ramsbotham of Kensington and continues to be associated with such matters from the cross-benches.

ACKNOWLEDGEMENTS

This book includes writing by people I have worked with both inside and outside of jails.

Written permission has been granted in all cases to use the examples, names and other details have been altered or omitted to ensure confidentiality and safeguard victims. Neither have I mentioned any of the prisons nor youth offending teams I have worked for by name, though I must say that I am indebted to the management and officers at the young offender institution where I have worked for the last five years. They have made my work and this book possible.

I would like to thank by name though, the Writers in Prison Network which has run over 130 residencies since being established in 1992. The WIPN has been greatly supportive of me personally and has undoubtedly sown seeds of change in many lives. It is a predictable scandal that it is currently in a fight for its survival and, if you find any of what follows useful, I implore you to support WIPN in some way.

Writing exercises like their drama counterparts get passed on, absorbed, adapted and reborn and a number here probably have antecedents in writing workshops I've attended. Where I have consciously included exercises devised by others I've sought permission and acknowledged this at appropriate points in the book.

Of course, this publication would not be the same without the work of my participants and I would especially like to thank the young lads at the prison who have been supportive of my residency and of my writing this book.

There is more to all of us than the worst thing we have done.

Michael Crowley

April 2012

FOREWORD

There are some words that you never forget, and amongst the most memorable that I heard while HM Chief Inspector of Prisons were those of the Head of Learning and Skills at HM Young Offender Institution Northallerton, who said to me that her main problem was motivating young people to want to learn. Like many others in her position, she recounted the dreadful educational statistics of the young offenders, better described as non-educational statistics, because they amounted to an indictment of a school system that produced so many with minimal achievement. To find so many 18-year-olds with reading ages of less than seven years, as well as those who could not read at all, let alone lack of numerical skills, alarmed me as well as explaining why so many of them had an outlook on life devoid of hope or ambition.

However, amongst this debris, I found a group of people who gave me hope because all of them appeared to share Winston Churchill's view that

> … there is a treasure in the heart of every person if only you can find it.

Building on what was there, or what was implanted by teachers in the YOI, writers in residence, or creative writers, encouraged young people to find their own treasure and exploit it. They also recognised that too many young people lacked another vital ingredient of hope and ambition, namely self-esteem. Nothing builds self-esteem better than personal achievement, which they were able to develop by encouraging young people to write stories, plays or poetry, for which praise could be given. I have always believed that their contribution is vital, because they are able to give purpose to learning, to previously rejected reading and writing, and so to improving other life skills.

I am therefore very glad to see Michael Crowley's book, which brings the work of this devoted group to public attention, because each and every one of them deserves the thanks, not only of those whom they have helped to turn their lives around, but of the public at large whom they are helping to protect. Quite rightly his story is not one of roses all the way, because that would not be true either of the young people with whom he worked, or of the circumstances in which he tried to encourage them to find and develop their personal treasure.

Michael Crowley's book should be a wake-up call to the educational system, which allows so many young people to leave school in the parlous position that he describes, and which creative writers up and down the country are devoting so much time and effort to mitigating.

David Ramsbotham

April 2012

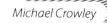

DEDICATION

For Polly, whose support and encouragement has helped make this book and much else.

HOW TO USE THIS BOOK

This book is designed to be a practical help to anyone working with offenders or those at risk of becoming involved in such activity. It can be used cover-to-cover or dipped in and out of, but I recommend that you work your way through the whole thing at least once in order to get a good feel for the range of strategies it offers.

To make it easier to return to your favoured exercises they are numbered and appear in boxes which clearly stand out from the page, like this:

Exercise 1	**Example Exercise**

Ask the participant(s) to think of their drug or alcohol use metaphorically: as an animal or another living thing or an object.

They must turn it into something that sums up the place it has in their life.

You might begin by asking the them to consider its qualities: the attractions as well as the dangers.

In between the exercises the narrative helps to give more of an idea of what can be achieved by using them. Examples of writing created in response to many of the exercises are interspersed to show how themes can elicit varied responses.

> He thinks he needs the river after all the troubled times and
> Years of going there. But he realizes that he doesn't need to
> Constantly keep going. He searches for ways how he could
> Possibly stop or even go once a week. He has thought about
> Moving away but everywhere he could go will always
> have a river. He's thought about avoiding it

An example from *Chapter Four*

The book progresses through different writing forms: memoir; fiction; drama; poetry, using random adaptations to given areas of work with offenders. However, in *Appendix 1* there are examples of approaches based upon particular issues which those working with offenders and their writing might want to address, such as:

- victim awareness
- anger and aggression
- drug and alcohol use.

In order to further develop themes suggestions about opportunities for discussion have been earmarked, although almost anything in the book can be adapted to, or turned into, a lead for discussion: Discussion suggestions can also be used in order to ask for written answers.

Discussion Suggestion 1

How does it help to think of your relationship to drugs/alcohol in a different way — as a relationship with a different thing?

Do you think you are a different person under the influence of drugs/alcohol?

Write a description of yourself in the third person when you are 'under the influence'. Concentrate on how you make the voice that is describing you feel.

THE CASE FOR THE PROSECUTION

1

This is a book about getting people to write and writing with them, and what that teaches us both. It has been written primarily for professionals who work with offenders and people at risk; a generality that needs qualifying here at the outset. Each alone are contentious terms, placed together they are a large and fine net that captures the serious offender as well as the juvenile on the cusp of a caution. There is writing here by individuals from both ends of the spectrum, though I have not said which is which.

We all have an archetypal lawbreaker in our head. If you work in the industry like me you might have a host, the people who need to be saved as well as the people best avoided. It is entirely up to the reader to decide with whom the following exercises and approach can be employed. It might not be for everyone in your classroom or on your caseload but I recommend practitioners cast widely. Indeed the exercises may be used with anyone, of any age, and have been, though nearly all of the anecdotes and examples of writing in this book do concern young men and women who have committed crime; somehow it's more gratifying to find valuables in the least likely of places. It's also because the point of my practice and of this book is to facilitate writing for the purpose of personal change. I aim to show how creative writing can be used as a tool in offence-focused work and victim awareness, in assessment and intervention. It is not necessary to be a writer to use this book, but you will find it much easier to lead the uninitiated if you're prepared to try the exercises yourself.

I've worked with teenagers all my working life, in education, the criminal justice system and as a writer. When I began writing drama

I was an education worker in a young offenders institution (YOI) and I couldn't help but draw on the characters and narrative I observed every day. Later, as a youth offending team (YOT) officer, I decided I wanted to use young people's writing to get to know the individuals under my supervision, and, as ambitious as it might seem, as a basis for making the changes I was supposed to. What began with a youngster bringing a poem to an appointment developed into the practice of using creative writing as an instrument of engagement, assessment and discovery. Several years later I returned to work in a YOI but this time as a writer in residence through the Writers in Prison Network.[1]

I'm into my fifth year now and, like many of the young men I see come and go, I'm convinced this will definitely be my last stretch. It is an institution holding around five hundred young men between 18-21 years old many of whom, even at that age, have been to prison several times. Visiting a prison regularly for legal or sentence planning meetings is a different experience from working in one, even on a part-time basis. You are immediately amidst prisoners' daily lives, and the regime that governs and becomes part of your life. This is acutely the case with officers who must impose the regime at the same time as building a relationship with lads whilst keeping their own lives at a distance. My residency has changed my view of prison, of my country and of myself. The institution, for its part, has valued my work for its own sake, has been supportive and stuck by me when the wider climate has become unfavourable to the very existence of such a role.

This book started with one young person in particular, a girl, on my YOT caseload whose mother lived in absolute fear of a violent man. She must have been as weary as me of the pedestrian work-sheets and my specious reasoning, so one week she turned up to her supervision appointment tight lipped and handed me a piece of folded paper that said it all. After I read the poem she asked me

---

1.   The Writers in Prison Network has been organizing residencies for writers in prisons in England and Wales since 1992. PO Box 7, Welshpool, SY21 0WB. http://www.writersinprisonnetwork.org/index.html

how long she could expect to be in prison for, if she killed her father (considering she was under 18, and she knew a good solicitor, and allowing for good behaviour). She balanced the cost, gain and loss and concluded it would be well worth it. I wasn't absolutely sure we could count on the good behaviour.

Giving me the poem was the greater act of trust. So I decided to ask for more and from other youngsters. The contributions were forthcoming and I began to think about publication, a magazine. On a prison visit I asked one of the most persistent and implacable young offenders you wouldn't want to meet, to write about life in custody, for the sake of those yet to arrive there.

Owen had left school at 14 but he was sharp, and he had enough time on his hands. Two weeks later 18 pages arrived in the post.

Monday

I get woken by the sound of the big steel doors slamming shut, as the screws come round and ask us if we want a shave. It's 7.45 am and it's fuckin freezing coz they never put the heating on. I try and get comfy and warm on the wafer thin foam bed and holey itchy blankets. Next thing I know my door is pushed open and the "breakfast" gets shouted into my cell. Shit I over slept. Gotta get ready quick time and get some munch. Still half asleep and wiv my jumper on back to front I wobble over to the canteen to get my two slices of cold half cooked toast, spoon full of hard beans, pink sausage and a bowl of lumpy porridge which tastes like cardboard. Me and my boys sit at our table n get joke n talk about last nights T.V. coz there ain't nuttin else to talk about coz fuck all goes on.

Owen (aged 17)

When I approached management about a publication they were supportively sceptical. You would be. Generally teenagers going through the revolving door of a YOT fail at school and many other things. Their literacy is often below par and their concentration poor. All reasons, I considered, to get them writing.

My other major reason was story. Conflict makes for good drama and children in trouble with the law have it in abundance: physical; emotional; psychological; in keeping with good theatrical characters. Many openly seek conflict at every available and unavailable turn. To what end? So they can tell the story later. They see themselves as caught up in stories, always the central character, the only character that matters. The hope is that they get the sense to see that they can change it to another story and that there are other characters with journeys that matter, just as much as theirs.

Creative writing anthologies by children and young
people under a youth offending team.

The first collection began as I often begin with a child, with their story. As with the piece below, it's often about airing grievances.

Behind the Lines

Behind the newspaper lines about me
Is an alright person.
If you read the paper
You would think I was a little bastard
Not the type of person to be near.

Behind the lines that make people frightened of me
is someone being paid to say that.

Behind the ASBO

there are places I would like to go

but the ASBO stops me going where

I used to go.

Why doesn't the paper ever print anything good

about people?

Sixteen-year-old lad on Supervision

Then the same story told from a different perspective.

It wasn't what was taken that really bothered me. It was the fact that someone
had been in my home, uninvited, in the middle of the night. The police said it
was obvious that a child had been put through the window after it had been
forced…

Seventeen-year-old lad on a Referral Order

Then onto the creation of new characters with completely new
stories in a different world, as far away as we can go, within reach of
authenticity. I produced four collections of young people's writing
at the YOT and many of the pieces, the best pieces, are monologues
in the voices of imaginary and detailed characters, a generation, a
gender away.

It took time and effort to get there and whilst the words were
written by the young people, they did not get there by themselves.
The following chapters illustrate the process of both oral and writing
warm–ups, from writing exercises through to text and from rehearsal
through to performance. I have also included suggestions for discussion that can also be used to ask for written answers.

By BV a 17-year-old lad on
an Intensive Supervision and
Surveillance Programme (ISSP).

I asked young people who didn't
want to write to illustrate.

Young people without much academic ability are often wrongly assumed to lack imagination or even sufficient internal life to create a fictional character with enough desire to drive a story. But young people are risk takers, young offenders particularly. They do not self-censor like adults. Particularly well educated and over trained adults. There is little interval between action and reaction, between instinct and deed. If they want to say something they will. And if they want to inhabit a character they will do so, without asking permission or inhibition. The absence of a policeman in their head can lead to much strife but it can also make for expressive and direct writing. I worked with a lad for a few years whose father died of a heroin overdose.

Lee used to MC (rap) a bit, scrawling lyrics on his bedroom wall, too depressed to do much more about it. I lost count of the number of notebooks I bought him. But he eventually filled one and gave it to me.

Face to Face

How would you like it if ya dad died in the local shop
Knowing every day ya got to walk that way
Knowing it every step of the way
Looking at the flat where he died
Knowing he got left outside
With a sign round his neck and a dog bowl at the side
Piss take the man's gonna die
People think they know what it feels like inside
Sarcastic bastards I see it in their eyes

My mother thinks it's one big fucking dream
She thinks one day he'll come back on the scene
If I loose the plot if I get locked away
I wouldn't want me little sister seeing me that way
Me little sister took way

My dad died of smack
And people think they can have a laugh
Behind my back
They don't know how to react
Face to face.

Lee

Even keeping a diary with a young person can be a good place to start. Creative writing sessions at YOT or probation appointments can seem an odd notion to some, but not if they begin with recording their point of view. I asked a lad to keep a diary with me about his anti-social behaviour order (ASBO) for six months. He wrote the diary at the office which suited us both. He had no one at home to encourage him and I could help with spelling. It also meant he attended appointments regularly for the first time, since the prospect of breach proceedings in court bothered him little.

> I now have eight breaches of ASBO. At least eight. It looks like I'm going to jail. To tell you the truth I want to go. I can't even walk down the road without getting nicked. My mum doesn't understand what it's like. If my mum had an ASBO that she couldn't be with her mates, I know she wouldn't stick to it. It causes arguments. She don't like me going to the shop, in case I get nicked. I'll probably be locked up by Christmas. Tell the truth I wish I was dead sometimes. I've been warring with gun men in the hope they shoot me. I can't do my tag this time. I got put on ISSP bail for someone knocking on my door. It's not even like I knocked on his door. I have no say in the courts. They do whatever they want. I'm in court on the fourteenth. This is bare true talk.
>
> *IB (aged 17)*

Undoubtedly I wouldn't have been able to get as many young people to write in my YOT without the promise of publication. Before the first magazine I can remember a number of youngsters warning me about the it not coming out or their work not being in it. It became a regular feature of the waiting room and for once some boasted about their writing instead of their offences.

Of course the problem is that the youngsters were also a regular feature of the waiting room, which begs the question: does any of this work? It works in the sense that it can improve literacy, self-esteem, empathy, concentration and attendance; but stopping young people offending, in isolation? Rarely, and even more rarely with children and young people whose lives are not well managed by themselves or anyone else. The work has to be part of a collaboration of interventions that inform one another.

Children and young people can be under supervision to a YOT from a few months to several years and in my view all contacts with the team should be learning experiences. I spent seven years as a senior officer in a team and worked for an agency in a number of others and I can tell you that for most of the youngsters most appointments were anything but. Case managers struggled to know what to do or discuss with children week in week out. Some even interviewed children (and parents) in the waiting room, and then hurried back to the computer screen, for that was the thing that demanded the most attention: the database. It mattered to managers because the Youth Justice Board ran a league table based on quarterly returns from each team's database (Youth Offender Information System: YOIS) and if you were a manager of a team in the YOIS relegation zone for long enough then you would be invited to leave.

Thus virtual contact with young people was more important than time in their company. On day one a line manager told me that a particular individual was the best YOT officer in the team because, *her database work was brilliant.* The relationship between the practitioner, the client and their file is a paradoxical one. The more time the practitioner spends updating the file the less time they can spend with the young person and consequently the less they know about them. So what, one wonders, is being written?

In this context I began to use creative writing with my caseload and was inevitably told I should spend less time with youngsters and more time with the files. Poetry and memoir began as a way of getting youngsters to tell me about their lives and the reasons, as they saw it, for what they had done. It then developed into regular appointment work, exploring victim empathy, drug and alcohol use, violence at home and on the street. It became a way for youngsters to get their work in the YOT magazine which we then used in secondary schools to discuss offending behaviour with children at risk.

Only about a third of my cases wrote for me and some of the young people that worked the hardest at writing were sadly equally diligent at offending. But there were definitely young people who stopped committing crime, got a job, whilst writing poetry and borrowing books (that they rarely returned).

I have wrote this short story to give a message to other kids and teenagers in a similar situation or even different situation to me; and the message is no matter what someone is always there to speak to someone and to express your feelings and [I] no that is hard but shedding a tear now and again doesn't make you soft, if anything it makes you even stronger.

I hope I have helped other people by reading this, just to show them, there not the only ones out there.

Anon

Obviously there's been a lot of stuff going on in my life and when I can get peace and quiet I can write. In prison they take the mick, they throw your work away. When I was there my Granddad wrote me a poem and sent it in. It was basically saying you have to be a fake when you're in there. You have to be a different person. If you're soft you're going to get what's coming to you. If people got into writing they'd realise. If they wrote it down and read it back to themselves they realise who they really are.

Dean (aged 17)

Long after my database and I wearied of one another, I parted company for some youth theatre work. When the residency came along, it felt like the job was made for me.

Unlike most writers in residence in prisons I came with baggage. I had been working with offenders for nearly ten years and in particular, as a former restorative justice worker, I had worked with many victims of crime. My other baggage had been sent on ahead to the wings, waiting for me to drop by. Former YOT traffic shouted salutations out of the windows as I made my way across the grounds. Boys, some known to my former team from ten and eleven had grown into young men, grown into prison cells (all those interventions). At least I had a head start. They were a little confused as to why I was there. They expected me to talk to them about their behaviour, their criminality, as well as their families and girlfriends and the importance of work. They also expected me to ask them to write and to read. They knew I had a foot in both camps. But they were surprised at how much I was asking them to write now, and the things I was asking them to write about.

Since then I have worked with a lot of young male prisoners ('lads') and have produced a lot of creative writing anthologies; memoir, fiction, poetry and book reviews. We've also written short plays together for stage and radio, performed them and even taken on a few scenes from Othello and Macbeth. Always there has been an underlying moral purpose and if it wasn't expressed in the writing or drama sessions, it was because I believed it was self-evident enough to occur to the lads anyway.

To be interested in a prisoner's writing without any regard to how the process might change their thinking and behaviour to me seems pointless. This has meant discussing crimes, grave crimes in detail; writing and rewriting about them; the planning and motivation; the commission of the offence; the aftermath on all concerned; their meaning. It is remarkable how little opportunity or requirement there is upon prisoners to discuss the significance of what they have done, particularly in a YOI.

In my experience, writing or text-based work is all too marginal in the rehabilitation of offenders and in this book I will show how it has its uses through specific examples and exercises. Whilst written work isn't for everyone on community orders or in custody, it can certainly be employed for more people than are currently engaged or have the opportunity to take part. Neither is it an occupation that merely indulges the person who has satisfied themselves through crime. It can be a more exacting and detailed means of asking people to face up to what they have done, as well as a way to spell out a path for the future.

It has never been difficult finding prisoners who want to write. From the first morning I walked onto a wing to hear "*What do you do boss?*", I have never been able to meet all the requests or read all the work handed to me. One or two inmates appear to believe that writing is the purpose of their imprisonment. That doesn't mean that the dominant ethic within the establishment fosters or even tolerates individual expression. The job of the prisoner in a YOI is to be enduringly on guard from oneself. Lads are bullied for writing; they demand my confidence and some leave their pads (cells) with manuscripts tucked down their pants.

Not surprisingly it is the prisoners who are serving the most time that are the most open and productive. The trouble though, at least with much of the unsolicited writing, is that it tends to portray either sentimental conversions or a reaffirmation of the code; though some it has to be said is testament to a quarrying for solutions.

> That's all I ever want off people: their car. I appreciate cars. I understand them. I see the reason why every drop of sweat that has hit the ground during the engineering of a car has done so. I love cars. Everything about them. The way they look, the way they smell, the way they sound, they way they feel, the way they drive, even the way they hurt when they are abused. It's almost as if they talk to me. I can't speak their language though so I take care of them, look after them, drive them the way they like to be driven, wash them when they are dirty and sad, fix them when they are broke and mad. I can understand why people think I'm crazy. They are right, cars don't have feelings, you can't make a car happy. What was I thinking? Some people call it an obsession some people call it an illness. Most illnesses have a cure. I think the only person who can cure this is me and I'm far from a doctor.
>
> *Roy (Prisoner in a YOI)*

As well as its efficacy, the other underlying question surrounding this work is the literacy level of the participants. Offenders, prisoners in particular, are commonly said to have lower literacy levels than the general population. This is true. However people in prison are not representative of the general population. They are mostly young men from deprived backgrounds and analysis that has looked at prisoner literacy has found that levels are no different from the general population from which they have come.[2] That said, at the prison spelling is weak and punctuation sometimes non-existent. My work is a means to address that. Amongst some lads in the YOI there is a depressing resistance to improving their literacy; they are content to operate in the argot of text messaging. It has been my experience that a curiosity about language and expression, to want to search for the right word, is indicative of a willingness to search for answers elsewhere. An expanding vocabulary doesn't sit well with the mentality of the hood. Certainly prison often improves literacy, particularly amongst teenage boys. They are more likely to be involved in education, to attend a library and to write letters. There are officially no phones or other gadgets to fracture concentration. In addition there are also exceptions to the generalities one can work with: young men who were undertaking A-levels or other college courses when they were went to custody. One could, if one wanted to, concentrate exclusively on the more able end. But that is not the point of the work and, exceptions aside, there is no doubt that difficulties with literacy and a weak reading culture are substantial barriers to the work I'm suggesting. Often I do ask prisoners to go away and write by themselves, often though I am in the room with them as they write, waiting. They read it back to me, listen to my questions and suggestions. Generally young prisoners do not embrace redrafting, which is why it is important to keep asking for improvements.

For this work to have momentum it needs to be fuelled by reading, as well as reflection upon what has been read. The offenders who continue to write are the ones who read something other than the true crime manuals and *Top Gear* magazine. In prison it is undoubtedly true that people will read when they wouldn't otherwise. But there are two major threats to this advantage, both outcomes perhaps of what Richard Hoggart has described as the culture of *relativism*.[3] The first and foremost is television: ubiquitous in cells, on the wings

2.   Christina Clark, George Dugdale (Nov 2008), 'The Role of Literacy in Offender Behaviour', *Literacy Changes Lives Series*, National Literacy Trust www.literacytrust.org.uk
3.   See, particularly, Richard Hoggart (1995), *The Way We Live Now*, London: Pimlico.

when your door is opened and in many education classrooms when you get there. Prisoners find life without a television understandably very difficult, anyone would. Apart from outside criminal charges and loss of several days' remission, the removal of television is the ultimate sanction in the YOI. But lads sometimes also complain to me of the stress this constant companion causes them. One lad once handed me 18 pages of dialogue between himself and his turned off television. Below is an extract (which is unedited):

Telly	You life's a joke. Thought you would have realised that by now. Sitting fantasising with your Top Gear Magazine. And as for that letter, we both know that's a load of shit.
Michael	Who are you to judge me?
Telly	You know who I am.
Michael	Well why don't you go and bother someone else?
Telly	I would if I could but no one else seems to hear me.
Michael	What do you mean a load of shit? Listen, I am gonna change. For Laura, she still believes in me.
Telly	No she doesn't.
Michael	What do you know? You're just a little black box.
Telly	I know Laura better than you think mate.
Michael	Okay, so what's her middle name?
Telly	Elizabeth. So, where do you think Laura is now?
Michael	In bed asleep.
Telly	She's in bed but she aint asleep. She's got company.
Michael	I'm putting your screen in mate
Telly	Don't! Top Gear's on in a minute and you know how you like that.
Michael	Just don't want you winding me up that's all.
Telly	I won't then. So who's gonna win the premiership?
Michael	How do you know about football?
Telly	I'm a telly, I watch football.
Michael	Yeh but I don't.
Telly	I know — I'm watching the other side in here. You know when Top Gear's on I always make my picture the best I can for you.

Michael	Really? You're off your head you are.
Telly	I'm off me head? Behave lad. You're the one that's talking to a telly.

Extract from In Two Minds by Roy (Long term prisoner in a YOI)

The number of books borrowed from the prison library prior to the arrival of televisions exceeded 22,000 in a year. The last figures since televisions had arrived in cells showed that number had dropped to 7,457. The library staff do all they can to promote books, officers escort lads day and evening to the building. But in an effort to keep the numbers up no doubt, lads end up requesting and borrowing much from the true crime genre, gangster biographies and autobiographies.

The very act of reading is an important step for these young men; many have never read very much at all. The experience of surrendering their minds to that of someone else through a text wasn't nurtured in some nor is it something they are prepared to contemplate. And many of them are fathers. But what is read, I believe, is actually more important than the overall amount. It might not be better if more prisoners are reading if all they are reading is rubbish; it might be worse.

A dictum that looks in the direction of something one could describe as a cultural strategy, sounds vaguely Maoist I know but it simply means acknowledging that many people, particularly young people in custody, are culturally impoverished and then acting upon it. It could mean for example, reducing the number of hours televisions can be on — some lads prefer to watch them all day rather than go to education, to watch them half the night rather than sleep. It could also mean that violent offenders do Tai Chi at the gym rather than bulking up. All these things in a regime are connected. What often hinders establishments to make such changes is not the capacity as much as a lack of certainty about their own judgements and province.

The prisoners appear certain of their values, contradictory though they may be; cohesive as well, whilst the staff are more diffident and divided, relying instead on rules and protocol to define boundaries rather than a shared ethic. The prisoners know that staff must ultimately win them over; that the state relies on reform as much as sanction and that rehabilitation can no more be forced upon them anymore than temperance upon a committed drinker. Each side is always trying to pull the other towards its moral orbit.

It can be difficult finding space and privacy to work with prisoners, I often find myself on corridors and balconies in dialogue about the weighty and the delicate, as do other agencies. Officers seldom proselytise about prison or prisoners. They see a procession of civilians come and go and let the environment make its mark on you. And it does. Long term involvement with the belligerent doesn't mellow people.

With prisoners I have always tried to look for the young man that once might have been, the student or the apprentice. With teenagers elsewhere, I now see lawbreakers in the making. I see my own house like a burglar, streets like a robbery witness and reading crime fiction is losing its appeal. The cost I imagine, of being a police officer must be high. It is a given that long term involvement in the industry can also influence one's own moral conduct. Daily exposure to immorality and amorality, the lasting and permanent harm that crime inflicts upon people, can make one defiantly scrupulous. One can also become corrupted; by the demoralisation of overwhelming odds, by long term contact with genial, implacable and contented offenders who sympathise with your plight trapped in an impossible occupation.

Many prisoners I work with return to jail to pick up from where we left off, sometimes within a month or less. But some have written back enclosing their work, saying they are working and one or two to say they're reading everything by Raymond Carver they can get their hands on. Maybe they're lying or maybe they're shoplifting the books, I don't know and the impact of something so ephemeral is difficult to measure.

Experience is telling me that this work is most likely to have impact during the period of desistance in an offending career. I have also witnessed young people stop drinking, stop self-harming whilst being involved in short film and drama projects in the community. It may be that they were desisting anyway and their involvement was a mark of it. But markers are important in personal change.

> You cannot be a writer and a thug. To describe how someone may be feeling in a situation shows you have empathy or an understanding of how actions affect other people, you are sensitive. I think writing really helps to make people more compassionate and thoughtful.
>
> *Jack (Prisoner in a YOI)*

Very rarely has anyone I have worked with in a YOI or a YOT ever handed me text that would be considered publishable. I say rarely, because there has been the occasional short fiction and drama that with some development could've found itself on a stage or a shelf somewhere. But make no mistake, the point of my writing work is not to pretend that I can transmogrify young offenders into writers, but rather that they become young adults who can write and read better than before, and with an appetite for it, possessing a different kind of esteem with more insight and a more considerate attitude to others. Small beer perhaps but it can contribute significantly to shifting an offender's identity.

Scepticism assails the approach that this book advocates and is inherent in the criminal justice system. Right at the outset the point was made in a YOT team meeting: *the problem with this kind of work is that it's in danger of opening a can of worms.* More than one education worker has remarked that there is no point attempting drama with offenders 'because they lack the social skills'.

There is a thread in criminal justice work that suggests we avoid the shortcomings in people who offend for fear of offending them, or perhaps for fear of the intervention failing. It is a sibling of the wider target driven success culture that actually avoids challenging people, particularly young people. Always we are told it is the institution that has failed: the school, the YOT and lastly the prison that they return to. Work with offenders like so much else in public life these days is described as being *delivered in packages.* But the tried, tested and rehearsed leaves less room for colleagues to improvise, to develop new skills and practice and it also militates against an individual, client-centred approach.

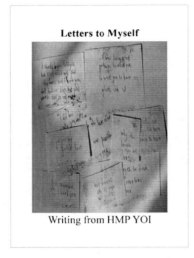

Letters to Myself

Writing from HMP YOI

First Night In

Creative Writing from HMP YOI

Front covers of anthologies from the jail: and on the right the
kind of image that can be used as a discussion starter.

Anthologies produced at the YOI are selective in their content and the work has usually gone through several drafts to get there. What pride a lad can take from seeing his work read by others on the wing has to be earned. Often they are launched at performances or readings in the chapel or library. Such events are crucial to opposing the pro-criminal culture within the establishment. Readers are required to rehearse and to perform their work; the audience is required to listen generously, with silence and applause. This isn't everyday behaviour in a YOI. Most of the drama performed has been written by lads under my tutelage and visiting actors and a director provide more than a little support. Three pieces have been subsequently produced in showcases of prisoners' work in London.

I also take texts off the shelf that find their own relevance. Shakespeare's Michael Cassio in *Othello* regretting an act of drunken violence, kicking his plastic bottle of blackcurrant across the space: 'Oh God that men should put an enemy in their mouths to steal way their brains';[4] Steinbeck's black stable hand Crooks in *Of Mice and Men,* forced to live in a barn. I spent six weeks looking at scenes from Timberlake Wertenbaker's *Our Country's Good.*[5] The text became a means of teaching English, geography and history, the process culminating in workshops with a theatre company who had the play in production at the time. It's more difficult to say (or measure) what lads learn by acting alongside accomplished professional actors, but afterwards they appeared to have grown in some way.

No writing is ever a waste of time. Children's writing particularly is worth it for its own sake. But for the professionals involved there is always the ulterior motive of assessment. The girl with the violent father I mentioned at the beginning hasn't been the only occasion where a young person disclosed violence and sexual violence through confessional writing rather than through a formal assessment. The purpose of involving a young person in a creative writing programme depends on the context of the relationship. As I have said, it is not always about the writing alone, and the degree to which it is about product or process will vary.

Evidencing one's work, not just through publication, but through evaluation is necessary. It is particularly important in arts work, because its relevance is often questioned and the change it makes is hard to measure.[6] Many in youth work and elsewhere seem to exclusively reach for the basketball to engage troublesome teenag-

---

4. *Othello* (II III 261), William Shakespeare …'That we should, with joy, pleasance, revel and applause, transform ourselves into beasts!'
5. Timberlake Wertenbaker (1990), *Our Country's Good,* London: Methuen. The play is based on Thomas Keneally's novel *The Playmaker*—itself based on the facts of the first convict transportations to Australia. When creating the play, the writer and director workshopped the script in various prisons and talked to prisoners about their lives and how they hoped to break a cycle they had not only created themselves but also that society had placed them in. It is this that is a key theme of the play.
6. There is substantial evidence of the post impact of arts work with offenders. See Arts Alliance Evidence Library research carried out by Angus McLewin Associates March 2011. http://artsalliance.ning.com

ers. If they do look to the arts it is often to music and rap music specifically or to physical theatre. The reason usually given is that we have an obligation to give people what they want.[7] Working with offenders is possibly the last context where that maxim of populism should be applied, besides many desperately want professionals to show them other ways to express what they struggle to make sense of themselves. To lack the means to express yourself is to be imprisoned wherever you are. Young as the prisoners are, there is a lot of writing about the past and virtually none about futures.

I will often begin a session by asking '*Why are you in jail?*' Many will instinctively reach back years into their upbringing whilst others declare the only reason is in the room with me. The current swing away from social determinism towards individual responsibility does not have to be at the cost of insight; and although insight alone won't change how people behave there can be little possibility of a different future without it.

> I am Ten years old IM in the Sitting Room every one is there My Little sister My Dad And me mum Just had Tea And me mum+ Dad Started on The whisky They every night After my Dad finished work like To have A drink. This night is Like A normal night ~~Apart from my mum is could Fomos~~ But It isnt I know my mum is court To morow I imagined That my mum wuud Be coming Home ~~8k~~ ~~that morning~~ she knows she isint comeing back. This changen my whole life She Doesnt come Back And my Dad Gets A new parther she doest come back so I end up in Trouble And get put into care when she Does come Back She Gets on drink + drugs And loses her R home which made her homeless which made

Dee

---

7.   'If I had asked people what they wanted, they would have said faster horses': Henry Ford.

People benefit because it's a way to unlock hidden emotion. It's a way of being understood. It's a way to get out of this world and into another where anything can happen. I've tried to write from a victim of crime perspective, and the truth is, I've never thought like this before. I've never even bothered about people I don't know. I've always thought, if I don't know someone, why should I care? Writing from their perspective makes me think about their lives.

Roy

STARTING FROM SCRATCH 2

2.1   The Uses of Autobiographical Writing

Not everyone wants to write about themselves. For some people, the last thing they want to excavate is their own life. Prisoners occasionally ask me to work with a new inmate, a co-defendant or a friend, who cannot cope with their sentence or with prison per se. I unlocked the cell door of one such lad who had been sentenced the previous week, he swung off his bunk:

> I don't want to write anything about crime, anything to do with gangs.

He wrote a short story set in the Manchester rag trade. It amazed other gang members and lads on the wing, who unlike him aren't serving 15 years. There are those that desire or who are compelled to look elsewhere at the outset, but most prisoners, most youngsters with YOTs or probation, most people in one way or another, begin by writing about themselves. In the context of criminality this is at the same time potentially both problematic and useful. You could be feeding an ego in desperate need of a diet, but also beginning to put it in its place.

Popular culture in Britain has become celebrity culture and it is unperturbed by criminality. It includes many ex-offenders or otherwise on its guest list. In fact criminality and celebrity have always enlisted one another from Ned Kelly to Mr Nice and the contemporary music clichés which lay claim to felonies to boost record sales.

A status obsessed culture intensified by personalised technology undoubtedly contributes to young people, young men in particular, carving out reputations by any means necessary. Thus a creative writing programme with offenders should avoid being sucked into the arsenal of a pro-criminal culture.

There are always a few prisoners who believe they are the reason for my residency, that I've come to write about them. They are big shots in waiting—behind a door most of the day(s). Other lads will hand me manuscripts, rough memoirs that prosaically catalogue the passage from home to HMP. Most prisoners I encounter though, have never written before, creatively at least, and are not sure they can. They want help getting started and the reason they want to write is because they know they have problems to resolve and they believe writing will help them.

2.2   Beginnings

Whether there is anything to go on or not I usually start with some introductory exercises by way of getting acquainted.

All writing and writing exercises I ask people to do are encompassed by discussion; in many cases it is the point of the work. I have included some discussion suggestions after exercises which I hope aren't too obvious. Of course you may find the discussion flows by itself and is hopefully initiated by the participants, the point of my suggestions is to enhance the exercises as well as the learning experience for both parties

Exercise 1   What's in a Name?

Ask the participant(s) to write their name(s) down the side of the page. Then to write a sentence describing themselves in some way, beginning with each letter. For example:

Makes playing the guitar look difficult.

I need to be on my own sometimes — often at the suggestion of others.

Can't stand heights or a lot of noise

Has a garden that he loves (to look at).

Actually not as funny as he thinks he is

Eggs in any form is his favourite food

Likes churches but isn't religious

Ask the participant(s) to write down:

A decision they made in the last week; a decision they have come to in their mind will do;

or

a disagreement they had in the last week;

or

a dream they had they can remember;

or

all three of the above.

Discussion Suggestion 1

Ask the participant(s) to think of someone whom they are fond of. If they were to write their name down the side of a page acrostically, i.e. so that the first letter of each line spells out that persons' name, how would they describe them?

What other decisions might need to be made soon?

Exercise 2	**Angel Heart**

You're a private detective sent on a case to put someone under surveillance: this person is yourself. Up to now you've only been handed a photo of the target.

You're in a car with a telephoto lens observing yourself across the street, taking photos of the target.

- What do you see?
- Describe the target physically: what they are wearing — their walk — their stance.
- What can you assume, just from what you see?

He looks like the average young black male, six foot one. Got his hair in plats, no facial hair, medium build. His dress sense is not the typical stereotype of a hoodlum although the way he walks and carries himself could be perceived as thuggish.

Junior

Tell me about yourself is an awkward question, particularly to someone who has done the rounds of caring professionals, it will get a disingenuous answer. I like to get to the first person through the third. Keep working the case.

Angel Heart (Continued)

Pick a day. Your target's on the move; where are they going?

They meet someone outside — a café or in the park. Fortunately you have a long distance bugging device.

- Write down the dialogue.
- From what you have heard — and only what you have heard — what do you make of this character?

Tuesday. He meets an Asian/Arabic looking male in Café Nero in the town centre. They shake hands and everything looks friendly. They seem like good friends. As if they grew up together.

Target	I've got what you asked for? What now?
Associate	Keep your voice down. Follow me and just play the part.
Target	What guarantee do I have?
Associate	This is not the time or place. Just keep smiling. Here take a cigarette.

Junior

Angel Heart (Continued)

Whilst you know the target is out and about, you go to their house and break in.

There is something in the property of great personal value to this person. It may not be worth much money but it is important to them. What is it?

- You've also taken their diary (a diary that belongs to you).
- Pick a significant day in the last year. What does it say?
- There is a secret in this diary that the author would rather we didn't know — care to tell us?

I entered the target's house and noted the following. The house was cleanish. No family pictures, of girlfriends or of himself. His bedroom was simple. He hasn't gone to any trouble here. I found some note books with poems and short stories.

Junior

Sadly it is not unusual for some people to have difficulty physically writing, at least at a pace that doesn't completely hinder the process. Hence on occasions I may begin by writing down for them as they feed me a line, but they will always write before the session is over. Initially I am unconcerned about spelling and encourage everyone to write in their own language. I want to hear the sound of their thinking, not a retreat into a bad impersonation of formal English. I correct the writer's spelling once we are into redrafting, thus in the excerpts published in this book the spelling and punctuation is often far from the original (although in the type-set versions I have tried not to correct things that would change the impression given by a piece and sometimes left the poor spelling intact). To allow people's work to go into prisoner's anthologies or anywhere else without being corrected would cause confusion in more ways than one.

WheNEVER I GET CloSE to SoMEbody.
for EXaMpIE WHENEVER I GET
SEttled and start coMING into
MY owN I GEt MoVEd and
have to start all OVER aGEn.

Extract from 'Arms Length' by Lee

Love is the most important thing, you arrive with it and you go with it anythin
else is just an aqaintence

Kyle

Exercise 3   **Diary Exercise**

Ask the participant to keep a diary for the next month. Ask them to record agreements and disagreements; things they have found funny; stories they have heard; achievements and setbacks.

Exercise 4   **Wouldn't Want To Be You**

Ask the participant(s) to think of someone famous with either the same first or second name as yourself.

- What do you admire about this person?
- What personal qualities do *you* have that they don't?
- What do you have in your life that they don't?
- What piece of advice could you offer them?

2.3 Automatic Writing

Automatic writing is a dangerously loose term. It implies writing without structure; tapping into the subconscious. It usually involves asking people to write down, without hesitation, their immediate thoughts in response to a particular term or statement, the urgency hopefully revealing unforeseen truth and perspective. It is a useful approach to warm up a writing session but for me its utility depends upon employing a few ground rules here and there.

I ask people to landscape their sheet of A4 and draw a margin one or two inches in from the left hand side. I then tell them that I'm going to call out a noun (abstract or otherwise) and I want them to write across the page. What is written has at least to be a sentence, I may ask them to include an adjective. They must write something, even if nothing particular comes to mind, it's important to stress that. If I'm meeting someone for the first time and the objective is to write something broadly autobiographical, I'll use general, investigatory nouns: *tomorrow; responsibility; hope; love; fear, etc.* If I've worked with the individual before or we have something specific in mind to write about, the nouns relate to the context.

Below are notes from an automatic writing exercise with a lad who was finding prison very difficult; he was frightened to leave his cell and couldn't sleep.

Sleep	When we are asleep we enter a world that is entirely our own.
Dreams	We dream on what is in our head during the day.
Nights	The world has rotated yet another time.
Tablets	They come in all forms shapes and sizes.
Prisoners	People babbling all night with the effect of rhubarbing.

Time	My father has become the whitened clock face to be the father of all time.
Home	A warm glow in your home, next to the fire, scorched tongue from a cup of tea.
Family	The two brothers argued and fought, the sour taste of blood ran from his lip.
Tomorrow	Their mum demanded the house to be spotless all rooms fresh smelling.
Thinking	My thoughts were never my own.

Jamie

I then asked Jamie to select eight nouns from his answers—which I wrote down against a fold in a piece of paper. Then I turned the paper over and asked him to write eight verbs at random, to see if, when we unfolded the paper, the random coupling suggested anything he could use.[1]

My nouns Jamie's verbs

---

1. This is an exercise I learned from the poet Pat Winslow. See *Chapter Six* 'What Poetry Can Do', the exercise Nouns and Verbs.

49

2.4   **Automatic Writing**

Exercise 5   **Automatic Writing**

Ask the participant(s) to:

Draw a margin down the page. You are going to say a series of ten nouns and they must write a response across the page.

- They have 15 seconds to write each response.
- You may stipulate that they include a colour or another kind of adjective in each response.

Which nouns?

- They may be general investigatory: *house, family, love, school, friendship, police, hope, journey, religion, faith, etc.*
- They may be specific to the environment and the writing session: *walls, keys, officers, meals, visits, letters, photos, association, nights, days...*

Since Jamie had tried writing a few poems already I asked him to take the notes away and make something from them.

Sleep

The world is entirely my own
Sifting the day's thoughts.
Tongues that have victimised
Watching the clock face that turns
My tobacco taken the hollow packet staring back at me
Fishing with the soundest friend seven years ago.

The world rotates another time

My thoughts turn from deafening to soothing

The father who has become the clock face father of all time

My mother who held the hoover more than she held my father

The warm glow of Christmas Day like a shiny football sticker

Nearly two years have passed

The good dream has finally returned.

Jamie

Asking someone to recall through the senses is a good way to start a piece of memoir writing. Dominic is a lad who lost his father whilst he was in custody and needed to write something down.

Sight/Image I remember sitting across from the priest and he was looking sombre

Sounds His voice was quiet but serious, clear and concerning.

Taste Eating slimy whelks at my Grannie's caravan at Coney Island.

Touch We would go out for walks and my father would carry me on his shoulders, with my hands around his forehead when I got too tired to walk.

Smell Of smoke and beer. I remember walking in the front room and the smell of smoke and beer would be in the air like a cloud surrounding him.

For the poem below I asked the lad to locate a memory through a particular sense — taste. He wanted to write something about his girlfriend and I thought sharing a meal would make a change. To build a picture of the occasion I then asked the lad to write a response to smell, touch, sound, colours and dreams. The smell wasn't the food, it was the new surroundings — the significance of the meal was that they had just moved in together. I'm always looking for patterns in any of the senses or across them: her tanned skin, the brown carpet, the dog and its mess, his girlfriend's hair.

Chicken Madras in Wythenshawe

Mango chutney and red onions

That's what triggers it

It gets my taste buds watering

Just thinking about it

Just thinking about you

The smell of paint when we moved in together

That new brown carpet

The sound of racing party music

The touch of your hair your calf

Sitting behind you on a blue motorbike

Your tanned skin your faith in me

Your hand in my hand in the hospital

My dreams are about the pink bedroom

Having a bath together and

Taking photos with our phones

Running round after the dog

Cleaning the mess up

Your brown hair your belief

All these things I still have

Always and forever

JK

colour	the royal blue seats and the deep brown wood.
Smell	the perfume from the women who handcuffed me.
Sound	the russel of paper, above the silence.
taste	the taste of the tasteless tea and the butty.
touch	the leaking ink off the paper of the indicrent.
news	I remember seeing my verdict on the news. I saw them ryting notes about me in the gallery.
question	the question of freedom playin on my mind for a year of remand.
weather	~~the weather~~ the verdict day was a hot day. I wanted to go home.

Automatic writing exercise employing the senses.

Exercise 6   **Concentrating on the Senses**

Start by picking any one of the senses — then a memory strongly associated with it.

* As far as possible describe the memory through that one sense — be it a sound or a smell, etc.

Repeat the process, excavating the same memory using different senses.

* Does anything overlap?
* A deep sound, a heavy smell; an image of light, a delicate taste?

The First Time I Saw My Cousin

The first time I saw my cousin
I felt the fragrance, I felt the freshness of her skin
Like a bouquet, it made me shiver
She was with her mother
A Scouse girl's voice, the sound of the Out
I heard words that made me feel at home
Sounds I do not hear in prison

Alarm bells, keys rattling
Straightners going off, a lad getting terrorised
Not the friendly kind of laughter
Hearing a baby on a windy day
Sounds that make me shiver

The first time I saw my cousin
There was a warmly welcome in the room
A ray of sunlight, a feel of delight on seeing a baby's face

The tiny touch of a child
Inexpressible, full on madness, beautiful.

All the touching in prison is always to do with violence
But the first time I touched my cousin
The feeling was great.

JA

2.5 Letters to Myself

I was asked once by a YOT to get young prisoners to write (anonymously) about the mistakes that they had made so that the material might be used with children at risk in the YOT. A number of prisoners were prepared to do this but all said it was probably pointless because they themselves didn't listen to the advice they were given. I asked them if they could speak to their former selves now what would they say.

Letter to Myself When I Was Fourteen

Yes Dom,

It's you here, seven years later, letting you know what's in store and how it all turned out. I bet you didn't see this coming. Your sister Nicola once told you "You can get a bad name over-night but it takes a life time to get rid of." You nodded your head and went on with your day not realising how right she was. She spoke from experience and now I'm experiencing it because no one trusts me. When mum and dad put you in the kids' home it was because they couldn't handle you. All those arguments, smashing up the house, trading blows with your dad, you should have realised then that something had to be done to sort your life out. Instead you thought it was a holiday and started stealing cars with other kids like yourself. West Belfast is a hard place to live but that's no excuse. Other people lead good lives. I know you're stubborn and don't want to do what your parents tell you, I mean; what do they know, right? Wrong!

They know more than you. I realise that, you don't. You think they only see the bad things you do, well that's because you do more bad things than good. Sitting here in jail I can tell you that it's the people that tell you off when you're fourteen that stand by you. You were more loyal to your boys than your family. When you're in jail all you think about is the years you have missed with your family, not your boys. Seven years down the line, what are you going to miss? Your twenty first birthday—that takes place in jail. Your sister Christine has a baby, Caitlin. You'll get a photo but Caitlin won't see you because you'll be locked up in another country.

Brace yourself—your father dies whilst you're in jail. The priest has to come and get you on the wing and put you on the phone to mum. She is crying and has to tell you the tragic news. You can't even cry because the shock hits you like a train, listening to the most special women in your life crying on the other end of the line and you know you can't be there when she needs you most. Your request to go home for your father's funeral will be denied. Too much of a risk is the reason given. So, your last visual memory of your father will be fighting with him before you go to England. You talk to him on the phone but it's not the same. There's not enough time to tell you about all the bad times ahead, and believe me there are a lot. Then one day you will start to read and educate yourself, do a painting and decorating course, hope to get your parole. If you do you will go home and take care of your family and be the man I know I am.

Dominic

2.6   Variations on a Theme

There are a few varieties of the letter to oneself: as above, from the current self to the younger or former self; from the current self to a future self and from the future to present self. The last scenario is perhaps the most useful exercise to employ, encouraging the writer to seriously consider the future. People in trouble with the law are often not great at thinking ahead; of building a realistic portrayal of themselves in the future. The discussion will be more important than the writing.

> I'm not going to lecture you I just think there are some things that you don't have to go through. If I tell you you're going to end up in prison you'll call me a madman. Behaviour has consequences. You think two to three years at college surviving on EMA is pointless. You see there is money to be made on the road. Greed is growing in you and the prospect of making tax free money blinds you...
>
> *Junior*

Discussion Suggestion 2

Tell me about an event or time in your life that you now see very differently to how you did at the time.

How might you look back on your life now, in five years' time, in ten?

How have your attitudes and thinking changed and persisted?

Another way to approach writing to oneself is through dialogue: duologues across time.

Tom's Life

I laugh in the face of the police
I admit it. I've done wrong

Who gives a fuck about life?
Keep your head up. There's more to life. Just give it time.

I will carry on doing what I'm doing now.
You can get a job. It won't be a good job.
Working in a shoe factory or making socks. It's a job.

I wish I was never born
Life gets better in time. Give it time. It gets better.

I run riot around this school
Education helps me out in life.

I live with my mum and that's it. I don't even respect her.
I got two letters off her on Saturday.

My dad threw me across the room
He won't be able to do that now

I buzz off my area because we kick off every day and fight every day
It's a bad area to grow up in. When I get out, I'm moving away.

Tom

The key thing is to be in the moment both in the past and the present. You may need to ask the writers to go to a specific time and place in the past; evoke the senses to assist them to write the voice of several years past. I worked with some young Polish people as part of a youth theatre project that wanted to look at transition. I asked them to revisit the night before they left Poland and reply from the present.

I am frightened of a different culture
You should stop being such a pessimist

I won't know anyone.
Then stop being so shy

It's a simple approach that asks the writer to consider which perspectives have changed, will change and which are likely to endure.

Exercise 7	**Warm-up Exercise**

- How old are you? Take the lower number of your age and write down something you have only done, once, twice, etc.
- A respective number of things you have lost and also given to others. Been given?
- Take the higher number and write down a respective number of things you believe in.

2.7 How Many of You Are There?

Pat Winslow is a poet and also a writer in residence in a prison.[2] Pat has shared with me and other colleagues a number of writing exercises vital to autobiographical work. Pat describes them as *body self exercises* and they are a richer variation on writing to oneself. For example, asking people to write to an aspect, or a part of themselves. It could be part of the body or part of the psyche, an addiction; anything that's holding the individual back. Of course, the affected part can also reply.

Go on, go to the off licence and get yourself a bottle
you know you'll enjoy it. At first.
You've done it before and you'll do it again.
Gain confidence in the warmth of my contents
What have you got to lose?

Paul

---

2. More about Pat Winslow's work can be found at www.patwinslow.co.uk

| Exercise 8 | **Me Myself I (Drug and Alcohol work)** |

Ask the participant(s) to write a letter to their craving, then for the craving to reply.

Continue the exchange as dialogue: the craving's goal is to trick the participant(s) into having a drink or taking drugs. The participant(s) are feeling vulnerable at the time and keep trying to change the subject, but the craving always brings the dialogue back to drink or drugs.

How can it be resolved?

| Exercise 9 | **Body Self Exercise 1** |

(Permission of Pat Winslow)

Look at yourself in a mirror. Imagine the person is a total stranger.

- Who do see?
- What kind of person?
- Imagine their past, present, future as different from your own.

How do you look to people who know you and the people that don't?

Do you present a different face/body language to each person?

Note down all the different 'yous' there are.

The dissociative approach to autobiographical writing can be productive. We are apt to reveal more of ourselves if we are outside looking in.

| Exercise 10 | **Body Self Exercise 2** |

(Permission of Pat Winslow)

Draw around your feet. Let one foot represent the past and the other the present.

- Write down all the key moments that have weighed each foot down.
- What's made the foot strong, what's made it hurt.
- Write down how each foot walks.

Draw a future foot. Fill it with things you want and believe you can get. Fill it with dreams, as well. How will that foot walk in ten years' time?

Young offenders often have poor non-verbal communication but I've always thought it can be overridden by a better use of language. In a young offender institution it's a given that young men will strut around with shut faces but what is more discouraging is the way vocabulary shrinks in prison to suit the confinement. Eloquence is taken as weakness and what few words are used are compressed before they're out. Crimespeak is meagre fare; a blunt and dishonest instrument that requires tackling as much as anything else in the arena of rehabilitation. Someone's response to new language can be an indicator of a preparedness to change on a more fundamental level, whether this is thumbing through a thesaurus, tackling a novel or experiencing Shakespeare. Lads who want to speak differently want to be thought of as different. Asking someone to look at how they use language in differing contexts is an important part of the autobiography.

Exercise 11   **Look Who's Talking**

Explain to someone the most important thing that has happened to you in the last few years of your life. You can pick any two of the following to confide in:

- Parent
- Friend
- Employer at a job interview
- Complete stranger

Compare the vocabulary in the two pieces.

- What if you switched them around?
- What other voices do you have and for whom?
- What is your true voice?

Write it!

Discussion Suggestion 3

What judgements do we make about people by the way they speak?

Their tone of voice, accent and vocabulary?

Ask the participant what 'their voice' says about them?

2.8   The Small Picture

When lads come to me in the prison with memoirs they want some help with, the symptoms are generally the same. The narrative is too broad, the viewpoint too wide. They seek to write about everything and haven't used a magnifying-glass let alone a microscope to pick out the details. The remedy is to select a day, a conversation, the smallest action at the epicentre of a bigger event. To help bend the stick in that direction I begin with some specific exercises around what they have touched and where they have walked.

Noël Greig was a playwright, actor and teacher. As well as writing many fine plays, in 2005 Routledge published his *Playwriting: A Practical Guide* which includes a wealth of exercises on writing drama. His exercise *Today my hand* is one I have continually used and adapted. Noël's exercise asks participants to draw around their hand and record five things they have done with it that day. He then asks the participants to put a feeling to each of the actions: *Today my hand stroked the cat and I felt calm.*[3] When you ask this question to young men in custody the limitations of their life inside are moved into focus.

> Today my hand opened a letter and I felt annoyed.
>
> Today my hand opened my window to let air into my pad.
>
> It didn't do much else. Everything is done for me here.
>
> I am like a child. You can't be an adult in jail.

It's much the same with walking. The prison has a regime and it includes movement. Deviation in any direction is not an option. Most lads cope with jail. Some lads cope a lot better in jail than they do on the Out. Many argue that things are working out for them. They feel sorry for me with my residency income—prison is fine and they have a few years left in them yet. Listing the places they walk to and the tasks their hands perform is one way of passing

---

3.   *Playwriting: A Practical Guide* (2005), page 13. Noël Greig, London: Routledge.

the penny that might drop for them one day. As well as *Today my hand*, I use *Once my hand, tomorrow my hand, One day my hand, Someone else's hand…*

Today my hand turned on the TV, made my bed, wrote an exam. It did these things in prison, for stealing from cars. In the future my hand will cook for my family, will work and clean and write.

Liam

The following piece either reduces or distils a grave crime into a series of hand actions; a sequence of close up images that bring to mind a silent film. Often prisoner's writing about crime and court and jail attempts to make it very dramatic, exciting; as if the writing is a consolation. This piece has the effect of evoking the mundane.

> I remember the royal blue seats and the deep
> brown wood.
> I remember perfume of the women who hand
> cufed me
> while I stood in the court my hand sweating
> I remember the russel of paper above the silence
> I remember the taste off the tasteless tea
> I remember the ink leaking off the

Extract from the original of the poem below.

Two Sides

I remember the royal blue seats and the deep brown wood
the perfume of the woman who handcuffed me while I stood
in the court. My hands sweating.

I remember the rustle of paper above the silence
the taste of the tasteless tea, the ink leaking
off the indictment onto my hands.

I don't remember the judge's speech after the verdict.
I saw tears in the jury's faces.
They will remember me asking them why they were crying
when they had just found us guilty.

You were going to sacrifice your freedom for me
I told you not to.
We will remember the smiles on the police officer's faces
the handshakes and the claps, after the verdict.

Today my hand turned on a television. It wanted
something else to do. I felt bored.
Once it put money in a charity box
held shopping for my mother,
pulled a trigger.

Z

> today my hand wanted somefing else
> to do. I felt bored.
> once my hand put money in a charity
> box.
> once my hand held shopping for my
> mother-
> once my hand pulled a trigger.

Original extract 2 from the poem above.

Of course the title 'Two Sides' is the wrong one. It's only one side and it doesn't begin to look at why this lad was in court in the first place. All the same I liked its sparseness and put it in the next anthology of prisoners' writing. It convinced him he should be off the wing and in the education block: a start possibly. He got there through a combination of three different exercises.

I'd met the lad once before, when he was 13. He'd been convicted of a burglary and I was trying to set up a restorative meeting with the victim but it proved too risky. Seven years later he was beginning a long sentence for gang-related crime. I met him on one of the wings where, up until recently, I've done most of my work. We began by both doing *Today my hand* by way of a warm-up and catch-up.

Exercise 12   **Today My Hand**

(From Noël Greig)

- Draw around a hand. In each finger write a sentence concerning an action; ordinary or otherwise, beginning *Today my hand…*
- Connect a feeling and a thought to each action. It may be an unrelated thought.
- Repeat the exercise using *Once my hand, One day my hand will, Another's hand once…*

Exercise 13   **Emotion into Memoir**

- List seven different emotions. Without thinking too much, select one.
- Think of an occasion when that feeling was dominant.
- Explore the event/time by responding to the five senses and the word 'question'.
- Who else was there? Who wasn't present?

I then asked the lad to write a list of seven different emotions (it's surprising how many people find getting to seven difficult). I asked him to ring one in particular and think of an occasion when that feeling was dominant, but not to tell me the event. I then did an automatic writing exercise about the occasion using the five senses and a question, as triggers to respond to.

Emotion into Memoir (Continued)

Complete the following lines (or a variance of):

I remember the colour of…

I remember the smell of…

I don't remember the sound of…

I remember the taste of… etc

You will remember…

They will remember…

Then he simply built on what he had, in a straightforward way. For example:

Fifteen Minutes

I remember standing in the arch of a church door
the sky was as dark as my black trainers
the night was as cold as a prison cell floor.
We were keeping away from the heavy rain of a winter night
the first time we ever kissed.

I remember the taste of your lip gloss
over the taste of alcohol,

one hand on the neck of a bottle of vodka
and the other hand on the nape of your neck,
warm and tender.

I remember the smell of shampoo on your hair
I remember the sound of cars splashing
in the puddles of rain. I will remember
those extraordinary ordinary fifteen minutes
more than a year in here.
My life is like a door won't you please come in.

LB

| Exercise 14 | **Shade of a Memory** |

Ask the participant(s) to choose a colour from a colour chart.

- What memory does it evoke?
- Was someone wearing this colour?
- Was it on the wall?
- Who is present in this memory?

Describe a smell to the participant(s): chocolate, oranges, grass, etc.

Ask them to think of an occasion associated with the smell..

Describe a sound to them: laughter, crying, etc. Think of a memory where it was heard.

What connects all three? Fictionalise if necessary.

Locating memories through everyday objects, furniture and naturally music can provide a context as can global events. We often recall when something personal or intimate occurred by what was going on in the news at the time.

Think of three of your favourite songs or pieces of music; of three objects at home; of three events you followed closely on the news at the time. Choose one of each.

For the music, complete the sentence, *I used to listen to this all the time when…*

What is the personal significance of the object?

Describe the event on the news.

What was happening in your own life at the time? Relate the two.

Connect all three in a memoir. Fictionalise if necessary.

The lad who wrote the untitled piece below wanted to express that he felt strangely untouched by 9/11 because his uncle had died the same week.

I remember a box of cigarettes, silver grey
smoked by my uncle
a week before he passed away.

I could hear the commentator's manly voice
the knock of snooker balls, the mild applause,
I don't remember who was playing.
It wasn't entertaining, but the man

who looked like my father with a moustache
was concentrating. His lighter on his left side
the spade shaped silver ashtray on the settee
the plastic cup with half hot, half cold water,
I've no idea why he drank it that way.
A week after he was gone.

I remember planes going into buildings
people running from danger
sirens and firemen
hysterical commentators in America.
We watched this in silence.
We buried my uncle the day before.

Anon

All readable autobiography is thankfully fictionalised. Time is compressed, coincidences become cause and effect; unrelated events become a meaningful sequence. After all, the text isn't what really happened, rather just one person's point of view.

If lads are writing prose about themselves for other people to read, I encourage them to fictionalise to a degree. I tell them to exaggerate a little, invent if you have to; engage the reader, invite them in. Their story has to have turning points and obstacles to overcome. Fictionalising here and there also tends to make their memoir work a little less self-regarding. It makes them think about the reader more. Of course it is hoped that through the process, lads acquire a better understanding of their past, in particular their own actions, rather than a gloss.

Discussion Suggestion 4

Ask the participant to tell you when they have 'fictionalised' or changed an account from their own life.

What did they say had happened and what really happened?

Why did they change the story?

Do they have someone in their life to whom they always tell the truth?

2.9   Autobiographical Writing and Health

Over the past 20 years a body of writing has gathered that testifies to the health benefits, both physical and emotional, of *writing therapy* for people suffering with trauma and stress.[4] A leading practitioner and researcher in the field of therapeutic writing is James W Pennebaker, Professor and Chair of Psychology at the University of Texas at Austin.[5] Through controlled exercises Pennebaker has explored the links between emotional experiences, language and physical and mental health. Students were asked to write about 'the most traumatic or upsetting experiences of their lives' on four consecutive days and the outcome compared to a group who were asked to write about something neutral. Again and again, in clinical and non-clinical experiments, results showed improvements in both physical and psychological health of those encouraged to address past trauma. Initially, many participants reported finding the exercise distressing and it seems to be accepted that the immediate

4. See www.lapidus.org.uk A UK based organization for writing therapy.
5. The author or editor of nine books and over 250 articles, Pennebaker has received numerous awards and honours. See James W. Pennebaker, *Writing to Heal: A Guided Journal for Recovering from Trauma & Emotional Upheaval* (2004). Oakland CA: New Harbinger Publications. See also http://pennebaker.socialpsychology.org/publications

impact of writing about something upsetting can lead to negative mood and physical symptoms. However longer-term outcomes both objectively assessed and self-reported show improvements in physical and emotional health.

It has to be stressed that the writing therapy was in addition to existing treatment, however a meta-analysis of 13 studies of expressive writing with healthy participants also found benefits to the psychological and physical health of participants.[6] Whilst I am not surprised that there is significant evidence of the emotional benefits of exploring traumatic and stressful experiences through writing, what do seem remarkable are the benefits for individuals with a variety of medical problems such as rheumatoid arthritis and asthma.

How then is this thought to work? The notion of an emotional catharsis is a common one yet this is deemed rather unscientific and unlikely. Pennebaker's own theory from a paper in 1985[7] proposed that repressing traumatic or stressful events requires physiological work, albeit unconsciously so. Confronting the spectre, transmogrifying it into written language, if not at a distance, then outside of oneself, lessens the emotional and physiological stress. According to Baike and Wilhelm[8] such a theory has mixed empirical support.

Another possible reason given is repeated exposure. I remember a playwright telling me about his research for a drama about the war in Iraq. The story was based on the real experience of a soldier who had briefly befriended an Iraqi boy to then find him hanged from a lamppost. The boy's body had also been booby trapped with explosives. The soldier survived the explosion but went on to suffer from post-traumatic stress disorder. The writer told me that a psychotherapy approach undertaken was for the soldier to repeatedly retell the narrative, beginning at different points, elaborating at

6.   Smyth J M (1998), 'Written Emotional Expression: Effect Sizes, Outcome Types, and Moderating Variables', *Journal of Consulting and Clinical Psychology*, 66, 174-184 cited in Baikie K and Wilhelm K 'Emotional and Physical Health Benefits of Expressive Writing', *Advances in Psychiatric Treatment* (2005). 11:338-346.
7.   Pennebaker, J W (1985), 'Traumatic Experience and Psychosomatic Disease: Exploring the Roles of Behavioural Inhibition, Obsession and Confiding', *Canadain Psychology*, 26, 82-95.
8.   Baikie K and Wilhelm K 'Emotional and Physical Health Benefits of Expressive Writing', *Advances in Psychiatric Treatment* (2005), 11:338-346. http://apt.rcpsych.org

different stages, slowing down the succession of images; the goal is that the memory of the dreadful event becomes familiar, ordinary; mundane even.

Baike and Wilhelm also talk about the *development of a coherent narrative.*[9] Through the writing the experience is placed in a context; cause and effect is established and a narrative running over a period of time is set down. The trauma is placed within a world. Gradually the author begins to distance himself or herself from the experience and becomes a reader of his or her own story.

Pennebaker and others have looked at the vocabulary of participants in relation to intervention success and even designed a computerised text analysis system. Use of positive emotional terms and insight words such as *realise, understand, consequence* are more prevalent with participants who benefit the most. An approach of my memoir work at the prison is to encourage lads to stand back from what they have written, often weeks later, and see the text as a reader rather than the author. Is this a good story, a coherent narrative, a piece that's of interest to others and not only helpful self-expression? This it must be said is where the memoir, traumatic or otherwise, is for the eyes of other readers.

Increasingly, I have begun to get referrals from healthcare, probation, and drug and alcohol workers of lads who want to write something with me but not necessarily for inclusion in a writing anthology. Their writing has a different purpose which is first and foremost therapeutic. It usually concerns addiction; suicide or murder of family members; abuse; kidnapping; incomprehensible violence.

If one is regularly using writing with people who offend then it is likely that some participants will reveal traumatic episodes and want help writing about them. I do not propose to open a discussion here on the role of social determinism versus personal responsibility in offending behaviour, but clearly moving forward for some requires examining formative experiences.

---

9.   *Ibid.*

Exercise 16	**Witness Statement**

Ask the participant(s) to choose an experience from the past that has had a profoundly negative influence upon them.

Ask them to write about the experience in the first person present tense.

With each draft get them to concentrate on a shorter period of time, to write in a more detailed way.

I am seven. I am very worried and confused. I haven't been told why or where we are going. I know I am going to Wales on a train. Looking across at my mother her face is all bruised and looking very upset and scared. My older brother isn't that bothered. I think he thinks we're just going on a holiday. I don't think this is a holiday. I am seven but I know some of the pieces. I know my mum is unhappy because my dad is a violent person and has been violent to my mum and she's scared and now she is so scared that we have to run away from the violence. When we arrive in Bangor my mum gets a postcard and sends it to my auntie to let her know where we are. A couple of days later my dad finds the post card and finds us. On the way back home me and my brother are in the back seat of the car and every time me or my brother say something my dad yells "Shut the fuck up".

James

Witness Statement Part Two

Ask the participant(s) to write to someone, whom they know well, explaining how the past experience has affected their relationship.

They may or may not want to send them the piece of writing.

Ask the participant(s) to write to someone who is unaware of the participant(s)'s experience, explaining how it affects their behaviour and attitude to life.

Ask the participant(s) to write a letter to someone who is now absent from their life.

Dear Dad

You may not remember me when I was a baby but as you left when I was just three months old I do not remember anything about you. I would like it if we could meet up and chat but that's not going to change anything. My whole life I have needed a father figure and I have had to look to my step-dad for that. It's a scary feeling knowing that out there is my dad that didn't really want to have anything to do with me. I have obviously [talked] to my mum about you but every time it's brought up in conversation her mind goes blank and she doesn't know what to say. I have been through some really bad times in my life and would have loved to have got advice from you. What made you leave? I am now nineteen. I've been kicked out of the family home, I've been in lots of trouble with the law which I honestly regret. I've been to jail and worst of all I've lost a child. The not knowing who you are and where you are is the most painful thing of you leaving. For you to make an effort to find me would be the best thing in my life.

John

I would argue that even when participants are writing about offences they have committed they are writing therapeutically. Lads ask to talk and write through the commission of grave crimes because they are disturbed by their own actions. Often they are lads who have also suffered past trauma. Either way my approach is to work our way through the narrative, again and again, revealing something new each time, making a note of what has been discovered and what has altered with each visit. I may ask the lad to write the narrative in the first, third and second person and to write in the present tense as in a monologue or journal.

We might break it into scenes; write as bystander, go back years to find our opening scene. An approach I stumbled upon is working your way backwards through the narrative. People predictably tell their stories chronologically, but some lads give as much emphasis to the episode of driving to KFC, as to the subsequent episode where they produce the knife. This might be because they spent as much time thinking about the former or because they are reluctant to think about the latter. Telling the story backwards tends to repeatedly beg the most important question: *Why?* It's also harder to leave convenient gaps.

There appears to be a hunger to repeatedly write these narratives; to place the memory outside of the perpetrator. Sometimes the writing is taken back to their pads, sometimes with their permission copies are given to probation and the psychology department; mostly they leave it with me and often want an extract published in an anthology.

Publishing prisoners' very personal memoirs in a YOI can be tricky. Bullying is endemic. It is the dominant discourse in the establishment. Conversation is filtered through a lens refracting it into subordinate and dominant waves. There is a code that prisoners have to learn: eye contact, accent, vocabulary, what humour is and what an unambiguous challenge. Whether you like it or not, everything has an implication about power and security, about whether your time will be purgatory or tedium. I worked with a particular lad still young but with years of institutions under his belt, who gave me a glimpse into the art.

Excerpt from *Sully's First Night*

By Paul

He looked like a vulnerable kid. He looked scared, pale, he wouldn't make eye contact. That's how you know. That's how you work people out here. We look them in the eye. My eyes always know what they are going to do and his didn't. His eyes were asking you to look after him. He was slim and he had a number five haircut. He sounded gentle when he spoke. No kind of notion in his voice. First night on the wing and he was tested just like everyone else. They test your tone of voice, they raise theirs and if you can't match it they know from that moment on they have you. The first night Sully was on the wing I was just chilling in my pad watching Corrie just like any other night. All the lads were at the window talking and I wasn't listening much and then I heard his pad number get shouted,

'Eh pad number twenty two. Come to your window lad.'
I turned my telly down and went to the window to listen. I heard Sully reply,

'Yeah who's that?'
'Where you from lad?'
That was Kev, always interested in new lads on the wing.
'I'm from Birkenhead'
Kev just giggled to himself.
'So what you in for lad?'
'Assault.'
'On who? Yer mum?'
Sully went quiet.
'What's your name lad?'
'Sully.'

'Fuck what a name. Who gave you name like that—yer bird? Hey Sully you gonna give us a song then?

'No' said Sully in a timid voice. Then Kev raised his voice,

'Are you getting cheeky with me lad?'

'No.'

'So hurry up and sing for me then.'

'But I can't sing.'

'Sing now or in the morning I'll come in your pad and boot you everywhere.'

Sully didn't talk back to that.

'Well hurry up then.'

'So what shall I sing?'

'Twinkle twinkle.'

So Sully started singing. His voice was on the edge of crying. He couldn't sing properly. I couldn't believe it. In the past I would have said nothing but I felt I had to say something, I felt so sly on the lad....

A trainee prisoner is easily identified by a few preliminary questions concerning what they've done and who they know. As in the fictional scenario above, they might even be singled out by some strenuous eye contact. Once discovered the job is to test him in the laboratory of the wing for the course of a few nights.

Another approach might be a genial chat during association. *Eh, Stevo here was just saying his ma's name is Celia. Can you fuckin believe that? What's your ma's name lad? Why? Just being friendly lad.* The novice hands over his mother's name and then all night directed at his window: *Eh is your ma fit lad? Can I have her number?* Her name is lobbed around the wing and dished out in the dinner queue and the showers and life is easier for the neutral if they join in. The targeted lad can only fight (and inevitably lose) or put up with it. As a spectator one becomes inured to the routine and it is hard to prevent. The perspective of foreign nationals on what they see as a British ethic can be illuminating. One remarked to me: *They are your enemy first always. Anything else comes long after.* Thus, disclosing in a prison magazine that your mother died of alcoholism is lowering the drawbridge and the person who must make that call is the prisoner himself.

Those lads that are prepared to publish memoirs about bereavement, abuse, shortcomings of parents fall into two categories. Those that know that no one will dare voice anything other than glowing literary praise and those that are past caring any longer — if anything the work is a riposte. What they have in common is a feeling that by allowing others to read what they have written about themselves, they are fighting back against the past. Psychotherapists might say it is an important ritual, like the scattering of ashes; that publication becomes part of the recovery. What I do know is that it tackles head-on the bullying pack mentality. It is therapy for the institution as well as the individual.

The following is an extract from an ongoing memoir by an Afghan lad who carries but does not generally convey, psychological and physical scars shouldered from the war and from being trafficked across two continents.

Part One: Baghlan, Afghanistan

In live in Baghlan Province near the border with Russia. I am eleven years old. I am without any education, I cannot even read my own language. There's no school, no college to go to because my father can't afford to send me to one. I am only attending a religious practise class every morning. When I return home I take the sheep out to where there is dry grass and the sheep fill themselves. I bring the sheep home at midday and help prepare the food for my dad and brother. The journey from the mountain grass to my house is an hour and my dad and brother are waiting. We unpack the food from the cloth — four eggs and two nans. In the room is my father, my mother, my brother Jonmagul who is twenty one years old and my little sister who is two years old, her name is Chargulah. Jonmagul loves a girl but my father can't afford to pay for the marriage. My father is a farmer, we have a hundred sheep. We live on the mountain side and the place is like a desert and the earth is a salty colour. Our house is made of the earth and is not that solidly built; when it's raining the house is always leaking. Instead of door we have cloth hanging down like a shower curtain. We have four rooms in our house. One room is for wood and the things for cooking. We use wood to cook because we can't afford any gas or other facilities. We cook once a week because we cannot afford to buy any more wood. As we eat the fighting is happening in the distance. We had heard this before. Whilst the fighting was happening we could feel the earth shaking and hear loud bangs. The bombs come from everywhere. We are surrounded by war. The earth is burnt by war. When the wind blows there are sand storms, then the Taliban will attack the American soldiers. The winds are so strong you think that houses will collapse under them. Today is foggy and windy and you can hardly see anything. We are all sitting down together and my father is giving a mouthful of food to my little sister when our house is hit. There is smoke and dust everywhere and we run in different directions and hide. When I return back to the house I see my father lying on the floor and he is dead. My mum is screaming and pulling my dad and my brother holds my mum to calm her down. I am in shock I don't know what's happening. I am crying because my mum is crying. I am helpless standing in the middle of the dust, the earth is still shaking. With our house destroyed we went to live in the mountains. We found a place to make a hole for ourselves and put our clothes and food. We lived in this hole. The weather is changing, becoming windy and cold. The month of October. My mother can't see a life to live, she can't cope anymore. I think we will also die because we have no protection here. We have a few bags of food and we are eating a small meal each day and we can't get any more food. Some days we are not eating and sleeping on an empty stomach. But the war is going on down in the villages and if you go down there then you are not coming back. We must survive with our food for as long as we can. I can remember the festivals before the war. People would make coloured jugs and bring parrots and other birds with them. People played drums and danced, some people brought horses to race. Some people made jugs from the mud and filled them with different coloured paper and put a bird inside. Then a boy would kick the jug and break it open and bird would burst out with the coloured paper. These happy memories are very short, like a dream or when you look in a mirror as you're walking past. One of my uncles was a Taliban leader. He was killing people, taking hostages, he took my brother Jonmagul with him. So now my mother can't see me being in that place. She sold the sheep and spoke to an agent and she paid him. The agent took me away along with fifteen to twenty men. I am the smallest one in the group, eleven years old and I am scared.

Hagi

The piece is still in progress as is Hagi's struggle. Part Two describes the near fatal ordeal of being trafficked across Pakistan, Iran and Turkey; of being kept in locked basements and garages for up to 40 days, of others in the room murdered or having fingers and ears cut off to extort more money from relatives. It is the disclosing of the experience to an audience that the writer most desires and finds most beneficial.

It makes me feel heavy having some things inside of me and it hurts. Because no one knows what I have been through or what is going on in other peoples' lives. It makes me relieved to share this.

Hagi

I read out extracts in education to English lads (who routinely attribute their criminality to circumstance) sometimes their response is derisory sometimes they are embracing and fascinated. Hagi writes prodigiously and independently in a language he is learning fast; he is now writing letters for English lads. The telling of the story undercuts racism and religious bigotry. What is important to Hagi is not only that he is able to tell his story but that others must tell theirs. He continually stops other lads and introduces them to me, asks them to write their story the way he has done so that others can read it. He needs that act of solidarity to help cope with human brutality.

My view is most writing, if it is sufficiently meditative seems to make lads less charged, less burdened. After a number of sessions you can see a settling of the mind; a change of mood perhaps. There is something curative about the act.

Mother in the
cave by Hagi.

2.10 Autobiography and Empathy

Of course the people in the criminal justice system who are traumatised the most are victims of crime and the witness statement
exercise would work equally well, if not better, with someone who
had been traumatised by a prisoner. It is also an exercise that can be
used with offenders as victim awareness work.

Exercise 17	**Victim Statement**

Ask the participant(s) to choose an offence from the past that could or did have a significant
negative impact on someone.

Ask them to write about the experience from the point of view of the victim in the first person
present tense.

With each draft get them to concentrate on a shorter period of time, to write in a more
detailed way.

Ask the participant to consider how the victim's thoughts and feelings about what happened to them may or may not have changed over time.

The characters below are imaginary. I cannot be certain about the events but to my knowledge they are somewhat fictionalised. The process was new to him and my sense is he wanted to tell a story as much as to explore what he had done. It's a potential pitfall to be conscious of when asking offenders to write victim narratives.

My Car

I awake. Where is Kate's arm? She usually has her arm over me, but it's not there. I panic for a second. Then...she's at work. Working nights. I'd like to stay in bed but I can't. It's Friday, and a pay day for my staff. I crawl out of bed and the shower takes my breath away. I like showers. 8.40 am. I take a white towel off the radiator, start to dry myself, knock on Sophie's door. "What!?" "Time to get up is what!" "I'm already up!" I can tell she isn't—but then it's the end of term. A holiday. Charlotte is coming with us; Sophie's friend. She's older and she's got a boyfriend. My Sophie is too young for a boyfriend. She is very pretty but too young. I remember when she was born. The most beautiful thing on the planet. I packed the camping gear in the car last night and cut my thumb. This holiday—this holiday is a bandage for my marriage. Let's hope it survives it. I drive to the office—I'm just nipping in to do the time sheets. As I walk to the locked shutters I hear a rumbling sound. Across the road a blue sports car. Two lads in the front. I can't tell if there's anyone in the back because it's got tinted windows. Drug dealers or yobs waiting to rob car parts from the scrap-yard. They're always at it. I don't know why anyone would want to steal from Andy—he's reasonable guy. I think about confronting them, but I don't have the bottle. Not much to do now. Just a few time sheets. Ten more minutes. Outside the window I can see the sun and it feels like a sign of success for me and Kate. I set off back home, I roll my window down and feel the sun's penetrating heat on my right arm. I turn on the radio and Bob Marley sings 'I'm a rainbow too'. I sing along with a smile on my face, and I am on my street before I know it. But something's wrong, something's not right. My garage door is open. Then….it's only Katie and Sophie looking for sleeping bags. We're finally ready to go. Shit — dog food. "I'm just nipping to the pet shop!" I get back in the car, and then out of nowhere, like a ghost, a car appears behind me, blocking the drive. The car from the scrap-yard. The same lads. The driver gets out walks over to me, he is calm. Fearless. Bald head, tattoos, tall with blue eyes that have seen a lot. He wears a black tracksuit, black trainers, leather gloves. "You can't park there, I'm just about to go out in mine." He smiles. A powerful smile. There is a voice from the other car. "Yeh well it's our car now mate — he's gonna move it." I laugh as if it's a joke. Who are they? I look at Kate. Her eyes are filled with fear. Where's Sophie? Hiding in the back of the garage her shoes peeping from behind the fridge. Now the passenger is out and stood by the side of the sports car. "Give him the keys mate" I look into the eyes of the one opposite me. "I'm sorry I can't." He pulls out a metal bar from his waistband. A scream. "Ray, give them what they want!" So I take the keys from my pocket, hold them out. He calmly reaches out and takes hold of them. But just at the moment of contact, my other hand grabs hold of his. "We are going camping, you, are not going to stop us." The bar hits the ground and his fist hits my temple. Blackness for a second. But I keep my grip. He grabs me by the throat. "Don't be stupid." "You're not having them." The rod impacts across my face and I'm on the ground. Where are the keys? Kate is crying. Sophie screams. My blood is on the ground. My car's engine has started.

Roy

The author has stolen many cars from many people. A face-to-face meeting with any of the victims is not an option. I doubt if it ever will be. The lad has much work to do, more than is possible, but the process of writing enables him to continue imagining. Of course always working in opposition to the narrative of empathy is the retelling of escapades for the consumption of peers, be it on the wings or on the streets. Crimes are recounted in prison not merely deprived of empathy but adorned with disregard. Indeed our adversarial justice system inspires a number of versions from defendants; for the police, lawyers, social workers *et al*, and judges. But once someone has been convicted and sentenced there is less point in writing down a distorted account. The monologue above was performed by an actor to an audience of prisoners and some lads made similar attempts as a result.

Autobiographical writing can be a necessary precursor for effective victim awareness work and, having had the luxury of sitting down with young prisoners for hours at a time over a period of years, I know that getting them to look realistically at their own narrative enables them to better imagine and appreciate the narrative of those they have harmed. In youth justice we'd ask children who had offended how they imagined their victim felt, before they were scarcely able to express or comprehend how they themselves felt about what they'd done. The database required snap assessments on *emotional intelligence* and *victim empathy*, that and much else on the basis of one meeting. Commonly, an absence of contrition or the inability to express contrition assumed an absence of empathy. There was also I thought an implication that these notions are static or consistent between people.

Exploratory autobiographical writing is not just about oneself. Many of the exercises in this chapter can be applied to victims, witnesses or relatives, imaginary or otherwise. In the context of criminal justice it is about self-examination, but it is also the basis of thinking long and hard about oneself in relation to others. Paradoxically, autobiographical writing is essential in preparing people for and reflecting upon a restorative justice process.

The Room

I go into a room with a probation officer
As I go into the room I am scared
Nervous and apprehensive
I don't know what to expect
My feet are tapping
In the room there is a man who wants to meet me
He's my victim's father
I killed someone he loved
But he still looked at me
Like he would look at any other man
That's incredible.
Then he started to speak
Ask questions I wasn't expecting
We spoke like two men on the street
Without no feeling of animosity
He even touches me
I never expected any of this.
Sitting in that room
With a man who should hate me
And want to kill me.

Anon

Memoir is as much about empathy as it is about ego, and empathy is the beginning of morality.

Exercise 18	**Baggage**

Think of an item of clothing you no longer wear but still have.

- Why do you hang on to it?
- Write down a memory associated with it in the present tense.

An object or possession you threw away but regret doing so.

- What is its significance?

- Think of a photograph from your past that comes to mind. Write about the day, the moment in the photograph.

Exercise 19	**Choose Three Scenes**

Divide your life into three. It could be by years, relationships, places you've lived, jobs you've had.

Take the first episode. Imagine you are watching it pass you by in a train carriage. Freeze it at one scene. Describe the picture.

The second episode of your life is walking past your window. Repeat.

The third is a silent film. Repeat.

Alternatively write the scenes out in dialogue — as if they were for radio.

Discussion Suggestion 6

Do you think some people are more empathetic than others?

Do you find it easier to empathise with some people more than others?

Why is that?

FICTIONAL LIVES FOR REAL EVENTS

3

3.1   Exercises to Create Characters

Experience tells me that people with a history of offending struggle to enter the lives of others (that is, in an emotional or psychological sense). Doubtless they themselves have less experience of empathy than most. Consequently in the longstanding debate over plot versus character, when it comes to writing anything fictional with prisoners, be it prose or drama, I concentrate heavily on character. Besides, writing that's handed to me by prisoners is rarely short on event.

Improving the ability of participants to imagine the emotional and psychological experiences of other people is the most important work that can be done with offenders. This can be approached both through fictional and real lives, indeed one may usefully lead to the other. Character and empathy work is fundamental to effective offence-focused and victim awareness interventions. The re-conviction rate of participants who have met their victims at restorative justice (RJ) conferences is on average significantly lower than otherwise, precisely because they have been faced with the human consequences of their actions.

Although RJ conferencing is now accepted practice, particularly in YOTs, it is still the exceptional event. Face-to-face meetings are often understandably undesired by the victim, or otherwise impractical. As a necessary substitute, practitioners sometimes employ role play: hot seating the offender as victim or asking the offender to write to the victim whom they cannot meet. Thus rehabilitative work involves looking at the world from inside someone else's skin; often real, sometimes imaginary. As such, drama practice that explores different perspectives is not uncommon in criminal justice work; for example the work of Geese Theatre[1] and Theatre in Prisons and Probation (TIPP). What follows are a number of writing exercises for character creation as well as for thinking and speaking as actual others. These may be used with people in the justice system and elsewhere. I will also show how the process can augment restorative justice and victim awareness work.

It takes time to create a character, let alone speak for them. The playwright Henrik Ibsen (1828–1906) said of his own methods:

> When I am writing I must be alone; if I have eight characters of a drama to do with I have society enough; they keep me busy; I must learn to know them. And this process of making their acquaintance is slow and painful. When I first settle down to work out my material, I feel as if I have to get to know my characters on a railway journey; the first acquaintance is struck up, and we have chatted about this and that. When I write it down again, I already see everything much more clearly, and I know the people as if I had stayed with them for a month at a watering place. I have grasped the leading points of their characters and their little peculiarities.[2]

Bearing in mind that our participants don't want to live with their characters for months on end, here are a few devices that we can use to flesh one out more quickly. Broadly speaking we can think about creating characters from the outside in, or the inside out, although the two directions are not exclusive of one another.

3.2   Working from Images

From the outside in we may be starting with an image, the biological from which we germinate the bones of the psychological and

---

1. *The Geese Theatre Handbook* (1992), Baim Clark, Brookes Sally and Mountford Alun (eds.), Hook: Waterside Press.
2. *The Art of Dramatic Writing* (1946) p. 32. Egri, Lajos, London: Simon & Schuster.

the emotional. Conversely we might start from an idea, a memory or a word.

Exercise 20   **Someone Like You 1**

Think of a face that is familiar to you. It could be from the present or the past, but it has to be someone to whom you have never spoken and know virtually nothing about; you just know the face.

Draw the face, *with your eyes shut*.
- Spend a few minutes on this, imagining you have a close up camera.
- Think about the eyes and teeth, their hair.
- What do they tell you about this person's life?

This is an exercise I have used and adapted at times. Its strength is its versatility; whilst it is based on experience it then makes demands of the imagination.

Exercise 21   **Someone Like You 2**

Now answer the following questions about the person in exercise *Someone Like You 1*. Do not worry about what you know, what might be true or otherwise, this is fiction.

- What is their full name; date of birth?
- Write down three facts about their parents.
- Who in their life are they closest to?
- When they were young (maybe they still are) what did they want to be?
- What do they do now?
- Write down three things that they carry on their person.
- Who was the first person they ever kissed (romantically)?
- What do they feel they must do before they die?

Once the character is up and running we can place them in a dramatic situation, not necessarily in dialogue with another character, but possibly alone, considering a relationship, a past or future event involving someone else. We can lay the foundations for a monologue.

Exercise 22   **Someone Like You 3**

Your character has in a drawer in their bedroom a photograph of them with someone else. Someone they miss.

- Who is it?
- What happened to the relationship?

They are about to meet someone; they are excited. Who is it?

They rehearse meeting them in their mind. Write the monologue.

They once believed in someone who betrayed them (or vice versa). Write the monologue.

The monologue below was written over a period of four weeks by a lad under the supervision of a youth offending team.

Of George and Spain

1.4.05

I'm gonna open a bar with George, in Spain me. Definitely gonna do that. George's idea but he's gonna take me with him. Know why? Because I'm reliable and I've known him for years. Since I was a kid. I hate my job at the dairy, but I'm just saving up money now for Spain and mine and George's new place. That's why I don't go out, and that's why I don't have a girlfriend. Can't afford one. Haven't got time. What would be the point? I'm moving to

Spain. That's why I keep doin overtime and more shifts at the dairy. Get paid more that way. George can speak Spanish, I can't yer see. Dunt matter though because I'm gonna do the stuff where no talking is needed. Plenty of work like that. This bar's gonna be brilliant. I've even packed ready for the phone call off George. Should be any time now. I'm living out of suitcases until I move. Told me landlord I'm moving out soon. I won't be here much longer. George must be too busy to phone. That's why he's not phoned. Must be sorting things out over there. Been two weeks now. Hope he's OK. George's mobile don't work over there so I can't get hold of him.

12.4.05

All prepared now. Ready to leave. George's phone call should be any time now. My phone's the only thing working in the flat now. He must be so busy over there because he should have rang by now. I've been asking all the lads in the pub if they know where George is and they say, they haven't got a clue where he is. He's not even wrote to them. Bet it's great over there, can't wait to join him. I've stopped the post man and asked him for any letters or post cards from George and he's heard nothing. Something must have happened to George, so if the worst comes to the worst I might have to go over there and look for him. But in the meantime I'm going to stay here and wait for him to ring.

22.4.05

No gas, no electric, water's ready to go. All I need is a phone call off George. The landlord has given me notice — says he wants me out by Friday. But I'm not goin nowhere until I get a phone call or some kind of response from George. A lad in the pub told me that George had rang, which is good news, but he said that George hadn't opened a bar and he's just gone over there to relax and get away for a bit. But I know he's lying because George wouldn't do that to me, I'm too loyal and too much of his friend. He's probably just told him that because he doesn't want anyone knowing he's setting up a business, because everyone wants to work for George. That's why he's only told me, because I'm the only reliable one. People want me out of this flat, the bailiffs are on the way. But I'm not leaving nowhere under no circumstances until I get what I want, and I want a phone call off George to see when I'm leaving for Spain, and when I get there I definitely want an apology. I'm not shifting until I get that. So if anybody even tries to get me out of my flat I'll shoot 'em. I'm beginning to get an idea that George has let me down so if anybody does get hurt or shot it will be all down to George won't it?

Scott, aged 16, on a Referral Order

The above owes a little to John Steinbeck's *Of Mice and Men*. It doesn't matter though, Manchester is a long way from California and there is a great deal of this 16-year-old's imagination in there. The monologue is based upon a man who lived opposite him. His curtains were always drawn and he left his house the same time each night. He was interested in him because they had never spoken to one another. I'm sure this lad felt sorry for him, but that wasn't enough to drive the monologue. It's the invention of the man's desire and the realisation of the betrayal.

Once I've been through this process with someone in custody or on probation I'll then consider relating the exercise to their offending. As a rule, the first couple of writing sessions with offenders are not about specific offences or victims (direct or indirect). I'm trying to get them on the bike to begin with, after two or three short journeys, we change direction.

The fear was like an open wound,
My Heart was Beating its head off!
I've got to protect my family!
My Body resists all movement
I turn the light on.
Everything remains Black & White.

Extract from an early version of *It's Not the Car* below.

It's Not the Car

The deepest sleep ever. Then noise like an air raid warning. I awoke. Darkness reassured me it wasn't a dream. I didn't want to go downstairs. My fear was opening like a wound. My heart was beating its head off. I've got to protect my family. My body resists all movement. I turn the light on. Everything remains black and white. My wife is safe. Where is my daughter? Curled up in her bed. I have to go down there. I have no choice, my territory is under invasion. My life is being taken over by a stranger. The top of the stairs. One step, nothing. Two steps, I hear keys. Three steps, I hear panic. Four steps, I hear footsteps and they're not mine. I see a bald head. He is fearless. I freeze. I fail. I want him gone, in half a second he is. I'm embarrassed, I let my family down. I have known Kate all my life and I have let her down. To other people he took my car. To me, he took my dignity.

Roy

It's a little melodramatic; an over-compensation perhaps. He has been through community penalties, juvenile and young offender custody; so far. I've been working with him for three years. He told me that he hadn't been asked to consider a victim's perspective before, which I find hard to believe of a YOT.

It is always worth questioning the integrity of work with prisoners. After reading a victim impact statement, writing can seem a frivolous indulgence, and in some cases it is. But as the professional, if you remain clear about the objectives and see the writing as one of many interventions over a period of time, then the use of creative writing can be a useful component in someone's rehabilitation. If it is worth undertaking cognitive and behavioural work with someone then imaginative writing is worth considering as an instrument.

Exercise 23	**Who's to Say?**

Ask the participant(s) to consider the commission of a crime. To write the internal dialogue as they work through what they are about to do.

Then to write the dialogue that *opposes* committing the crime; as if it was also their point of view.

Give the different voices created a different style or place them differently in the piece.

The piece below emerged from an open discussion with three lads about the craft of burglary; their methods; experiences and sense of achievement. It is necessary to see one half of a picture as clearly as possible in order to try and complete it.

A bungalow a patio
Double glazing double garage
Big garden, I've seen
The children's trampoline

> *Burglary is a stupid thing*

I'm only fifteen
And I buzz when I do a graft.

> *Does this feel right to you?*
> *It doesn't feel like anything to me*

Go in the through the back door
Go up some steps go down some
Go for the car keys
The money the jewellery

> *It's not your property*
> *It's not your stuff to touch*

A TV and a laptop

It soon will be

> *There's a family photo*
> *Playing football on a beach*
> *Wedding pictures on the wall*

I turn away from the photos
What's this, in this jar, money?
Ashes and a plaque
An amateur would leave the house
And not come back
Not me I'm on a mission

> *That laptop could be the child's*

Well I've been in care all my life

> *And is this the answer?*

I hardly get to see my family
This is all I know
This is all I was taught.

> *There's a baby seat in that car*

A burglar has to be fearless and heartless

> *They must have saved up for it all*

They're insured aren't they?
Job done for another day

> **Why us?**

It was just your turn
Back out tomorrow

> **What have we done?**

Hope I didn't leave my DNA

> *This is their house*
> *This is their lives*
> *Where did we go wrong?*
> *This is their pride*

Burglary for me
Is just a business

> **This will stay with us**

My nine to five

> **Like a stain**

Going into peoples' houses

Makes me feel proud

Liam and Stuart

Progress can only be made in this kind of work with lads who are receptive to it. Blindingly obvious, yet journalists and politicians talk of prison not working as if they were industrial units manufacturing citizens.

> Prison works if you want it to work and let it work. When I first came to jail I didn't care, however now I do. My eyes have been opened to how victims must feel. I've learned to think about the consequences for everyone not just myself. I have matured and started reading and writing things true and false in a fiction format. I've been made to think on a cognitive therapy course.

Ryan, prisoner in a YOI

Rehabilitation is not something done to someone as punishment is; people must participate. An offending career is described by criminologists as being divided into periods of onset, persistence and desistance. The effectiveness of any intervention depends on many things, not least the stage in the offending career, and the context in which it is delivered. In my experience of working in both the community and custody, this kind of work gets a better response in the latter world. People in prison are usually bored; they welcome the challenge and the distraction from the regime.

Detailed character work is worth undertaking regardless of whether it leads directly to the voice of a victim. It encourages empathy and I know from experience that trying to write from a victim's point of view will occur to lads once they have inhabited other voices; I never asked Roy to write his victim's monologue, he handed it to me after we wrote a few pieces of drama that were nothing to do with crime. There is a school of thought that argues that in order to understand any given individual crime, it is necessary to understand the society in which it has occurred. In a society that increasingly fosters a self-regarding outlook, writing through the eyes of others is worth doing with anyone, especially the young.

Presenting a photograph to someone usually gets results. A fair bit of preliminary work is staring you in the face. Although you're giving the writer a head start there are still lots of ways to make exercises based on photographs quirky and challenging. If you are planning on a publication that includes the photos then you may need to consider copyright at the outset. It's one of the reasons I often use my own. But the one below was taken by the boy's mother. She thought it was the last time she would see her 14-year-old son alive and gave it to the *Bristol Evening Post* who put it on their front page as a warning against car crime. It is reproduced here with kind permission of Avon and Somerset Constabulary who subsequently included it in a car crime work book. When police went to the mother's house a year after it was taken to ask if they could use it they were introduced to her wheelchair bound son who gave his permission.

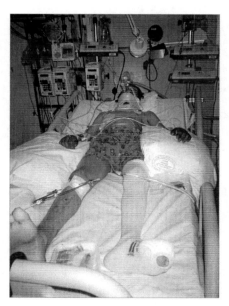

Reproduced by kind permission of
Avon and Somerset Constabulary

I used the photograph as a writing tool with young people who had committed car crime.

The News

The monitors are helpless now. The monitors have switched themselves off and switched him off. He doesn't seem any different; he was only a corpse when he came. Hasn't changed in two weeks. Hasn't moved. Doesn't look human anymore. I'm on my own with the dead. The nurses have turned their backs on Death and left me to tell his parents. I'm scared. Biting my nails because I have never had to do something as serious as this before. I want this to be over but it's the most important news his parents are going to hear. The room is dead, like the boy. There are lots of machines but they have gone silent. I am stood in the room with the dead and I am about to tell his parents. I enter the corridor, I'm all alone, there is no life in sight. There is a light above my head flickering on and off, like the boy was. I walk down the corridor and I can see the boy's parents up ahead me. They look terrified of waiting. I get closer. I can feel my heart beat getting faster and faster. I come into contact with his parents. Soon as they see me they stand up. They look poor by the clothes they're wearing. As I'm about to tell them the dreadful news, I can taste antiseptic in my mouth. As I open my mouth to tell them I try and speak but nothing comes out. His parents watch. I see a tear drop from the boy's mother's eye. I open my mouth again and this time, thankfully, I tell them the news that their son is dead. His mother drops to the ground screaming. Now the boy's father picks her up and they are both crying. I stand there and it feels like it's all my fault. All this, because the boy got in the stolen car.

Kieran

I was Kieran's YOT officer. He had been in stolen car that had partly demolished a garden wall. As part of his programme I asked him to come to the local Road Peace Garden with me. Road Peace is run by bereaved victims of road crime and the charity campaigns for improved road safety.[3] Kieran helped tidy up the memorial gar-

---

3. http://www.roadpeace.org Road Peace is the national charity for road crash victims and an independently funded membership organization. Members include those who have been bereaved or injured in road crashes and also who are concerned about road danger. It was given the Charity of the Year Award by *The Guardian* in 2008.

den and spent some time listening to a mother who had lost her daughter. A fortnight later he helped out at the annual memorial service, setting up and serving tea and coffee. In the centre of the Unitarian Church was placed a tree on which, at the end of the service, people placed cardboard leaves inscribed with the name of their lost loved ones. The lad was obviously moved by the palpable grief in the room. Soon after that he came to the office and I asked him if would like to do some writing, which he said he wanted to do *for the Road Peace lady*. Initially we looked at some photographs of the remains of the wall and then we looked at the workbook. He doesn't quite manage to carry the voice of the junior doctor throughout, but writing in the present tense gives the piece real drama. It was either the photo or his instincts that prompted that.

Monologue is a good form to begin writing with someone who hasn't written much before or who lacks confidence, because a voice, internal or otherwise, usually needs to avoid any attempt at Standard English. Photo collection-wise the *Working with Men*[4] series is excellent; look for the male image photo pack on their website which has individual as well as relationship shots; but they are of course just of men. Taking one's own photographs can be fun, you control the subject matter and if you are working in the community it's something you can involve the people you're working with in (risk management included).

---

4. www.workingwithmen.org The ethos of Working With Men is to develop and implement support projects that benefit the development of men and boys, and also seek to raise awareness of issues impacting upon men and boys in addition to trying to gain a greater understanding of the underlying issues behind male behaviour.

Exercise 24   **Interpretations**[5]

Ask the participant(s) to consider how different people might view the subject depending on who they were. For example regarding the image of the pedestrian below: a young woman feels sorry for the old man; the sick man envies him; the young boy thinks of his grandfather and smiles, etc, etc.

Where is the subject of the photograph going, what are they thinking about?

The homeless man thinks he going home to a warm house and family.

The rich lady thinks he is going home to a cold empty house, etc, etc.

Lastly, what is the truth?

Ask the participant(s) to write, where the character is going, where they have been and what they have been thinking, in the first person.

The old man is heading home. He is lonely now. His life is quiet. He wonders about the future as he looks at the gutter underneath his feet. He is a strong boned man—a construction worker when he was younger. His love life was long and strong and honest. He stood by his love.

Hagi.

---

5.   Adapted from Pat Winslow's exercise with her kind permission.

Discussion Suggestion 7 and Exercise Development

Ask the participant(s) how they think different people might see them on an average day.

Get them to write it: the elderly person; the police officer; the shopkeeper; the youth worker.

Are any of the perceptions true?

Exercise 25   **Take a Photograph of an Individual**

Someone they know well has something to tell them, a revelation.

Write to the person in the photograph as if you are that someone with that news.

Or

The individual in the photograph has some news for someone else. Who and what?

Or

The person in the photograph is in love.

Write a love letter that says it all but that they cannot send.

Exercise 26   Take a Photograph of a Couple

Ask the participant(s) to imagine they are one of the couple.

Ask them to describe the relationship in some detail: how long they have known each other etc.

- Why are they meeting?

As a character they feel the other person is hiding something from them.

- How can they tell?
- What might it be?

Or

You are one of the couple. Something the other person has said is significant to you, but you didn't raise it at the time because you didn't want an argument. It is after the meeting and you are driving home alone.

- Now say what you wanted to say.

Discussion Suggestion 8 and Exercise Development

How can we tell when someone is hiding something?

How does our voice and body language alter?

Ask the participant(s) if they have been in a situation when they withheld something important from someone.

Ask them to consider writing a monologue addressing that someone now — but only as an exercise.

A major advantage of creating characters in this way is that we can immediately be with someone from a different era, gender or culture. We can prompt historical fiction, ghost stories or fantasy. Photographs of a different world open up discussions on backstory, lines of enquiry beyond the dreary now, and they can be a creative and effective way to tackle issues about such matters as race and diversity. The next photograph is nearly always initially dramatised by young prisoners as a telephone conversation about people-trafficking. The work to shift the interpretations towards something mundane, personal and intimate is worth doing for reasons other than the writing it produces.

Exercise 27   **It's Not What it Looks Like**

Present the participant(s) with a group photograph. Ask them what their immediate response is to who the people are; their backgrounds, social status, etc; what is being said, relationships, hierarchy, etc.

Now ask them to subvert their instincts and describe the scene in the photograph in the opposite terms.

Giving the participant less than half the picture demands more of their imagination. Present your participants with images at a distance from imaginary characters, giving them space to work, evidence of a life in context, something that might serve to spark the counter-intuitive. You'll know when you see it.

Boots in Woodland
courtesy Martyn
Young

This tells me poverty. A house close by. Three kids. A dog called Toby. The parents don't look after the kids; they send them to do the shopping. Toby is their best friend. A sibling. The shoe belonged to the dad who's dead. It's behind the shed and his stuff is in that shed. The children are not allowed to go in that shed. The children don't know the shoe is there. If they found it they'd treasure it.

Roy

It is telling that even when images are used that are remote from the lads' environments and experiences, the written response remains anchored in their own circumstances

The keys to a piano are like the stages of life. A long high note signifies all the good points in one's life: spending time with your mother, father, son, daughter. Anyone special to you. Then we hit the deep note, the sound of death on the horizon. You play your deep chords to shout the anger and depression begging to get out of your soul. The keys are hit hard and the echo fills the room and gives you goose bumps. I may only be thirteen, but if I am going through this then there must be others that are.

Jamie

The Oriel Window in the Great Hall. Reproduced with the kind permission of Mrs Sharon Jones (Director) of Samlesbury Hall, Preston.

Portraits and paintings take us to before and beyond the photograph and can evoke mood more readily. They are a window into historical monologue, thus an opportunity to encourage an interest in history. The portrait which follows is of Francis Barber (Dr Johnson's servant) reproduced here with kind permission of the Dr Johnson House Trust.

I miss her. If only I could touch her hair, smell her skin feel her soft face for one last time. This pain I feel will be with me forever…

Michael

Francis Barber (1735–
1801). Permission Dr
Johnson House Trust.

When I think of home I think of all I have missed. I missed my sister growing up and I have missed walking along the beaches to gather fruit and firewood for the family. I miss the blazing sun and dream of the day I was taken away from my homeland. A small boy made to feel smaller by the size of the ship.

'Why did my master request this painting?'

'It's for your birthday, didn't you know?'

'Then I want it sent home to my island, so everyone can see.'

Thomas

3.3   Postcards from Strangers

Anyone who gets into the habit of leading creative writing sessions should enlist the tangible assistance of a series of strange and inspirational items. I have a collection of old postcards purchased at antique fairs and junk shops, some going back 50 years. You'd be surprised at the missives you find amongst 'Having a lovely time'. Betrothals; illness; threats; engagement regrets; my favourite just says: '*You are a miserable wretch*'. It was sent second class from Harrogate.

Exercise 28	**Between the Lines**

Read an old postcard written by a stranger (preferably long gone).

What can you tell about the author…from the handwriting, the message, where it's from and to whom?

Guess their age, their occupation, their wealth and status. How do they feel about the person they have written to?

Develop the relationship imaginatively.

Write a much longer paragraph to the addressee, then a reply.

3.4   Handling Property

There is a memorable poem by Simon Armitage entitled 'About His Person' from his collection *Kid*.[6] The poem is comprised of couplets listing objects found on a body. It's the final poem in the collection and the items serve as a guide and testament to *Kid's* central character, Robinson.

I was always looking for ways to introduce poetry into my practice as a YOT officer and I managed to develop a group work off the back of the text. I would get the group to read the poem and then tell me what they could deduce about the dead man's life from the objects. I would then pass round a bag in which I had placed certain things (medication, appointment cards, lipstick, a photograph) inviting each member of the group to pick an object and tell us what it revealed about the owner. Gradually the group would build a character; someone with relationships and a past. Some of the objects

---

6. *Kid* (1992), Simon Armitage, London: Faber & Faber.

were quite arbitrary but generally I was introducing the group to someone vulnerable or with a vulnerable dependant. I would then ask the group, having met the bag's owner, if they could then snatch it or steal it from a car, etc? Some said they wouldn't, some were candid and said they would but find it more difficult and feel guiltier afterwards. It wasn't the answer I was looking for but it was the answer I had to work with. It also reminds one that rehabilitation is a balance of deterrence and persuasion.

Exercise 29 **About Their Person**

Place up to ten items in a bag. These should be small enough that they could be carried around (hand cream; memory stick; iPod; glasses; a book; a shopping list; a note pad with some entries, etc.)

Now ask the participant(s) to select the items one at a time and use them to build a biography of the owner.

Exercise Development

Ask the participant(s) to think of an object that they would add which would alter the characterization of the bag's owner.

Introduce two new items. These have also been found in the bag but the rule is they belong to someone else.

Who?

What is their relationship to the bag's owner and why are they in the bag?

Exercise 30   **Buttons**

(Kind permission of Pat Winslow)

Have a container of buttons of varying sizes and colours available for the group. Ask each person to choose one. Ask the following questions and get everyone to write their thoughts down.

In appearance, what does it remind you of?

How does it feel (close your eyes for this one) each side, the edges, the middle.

What noise does it make? What does it look like; colours; shape; shadows; light or heavy? Where might it have come from?

Who last fingered it? When was it last worn, on what? What has it heard? What did this button person do on a Sunday afternoon?

Write the poem or a story about the button person.

Discussion Suggestion 9

Is it worse to steal from someone you know (even vaguely) than someone you don't?

What are the consequences of stealing from people who know you?

It depends on the relationship. I have stolen from people I know, but not anyone I liked. Just somebody I knew. And I have stolen off someone who has wronged me. If you steal off someone you know — you have to see the emotional fallout. If it's someone random you don't have to face that. Everyone has a conscience — it's just whether we choose to listen to it or not.

Ryan

3.5 Character as Trait

Characterization can just as easily be approached (some might argue should be approached) through ascribing behaviour or traits before we know anything else about a character.

> Jack Sparrow is a rebel, self-absorbed, selfish, will risk his life for greed and he's funny and intelligent. I'm very self-absorbed. Dr Jekyll is addicted and longs to be someone else and so I do. James Bond is self-righteous, suave, strong, intelligent and a patriot. I am also a patriot.
>
> *Josh (aged 18)*

It's an approach that can readily be turned into a discussion about the writer.

Exercise 31   Devils and Angels We Know

Ask the participant(s) to think of at least three well-known fictional characters, from television, film or literature. Get them to write down their qualities as character traits — as many as you can.

Ask the participant(s) what would an observer say were their character traits — if they were observed over the last month, year, five years?

Discussion Suggestion 10

Do we keep our character traits forever?

How and why might we adopt new ones?

Exercise 32   **The Good and Bad in Everyone**

Ask the participant(s) to think of someone they know but don't particularly like. Write down a list of this person's qualities.

Now ask the participant(s) to write down a couple of strengths and weaknesses in themselves.

Create a character based on the above but they must be a different age, background, gender to themselves.

3.6   Character as Motive

Playwright Tim Fountain has written a useful book entitled *So You Want to be A Playwright?*[7] Tim describes character as *decision under pressure*. Of course in the world of dramatic fiction we expect our protagonists to overcome every obstacle, internal and external, for the sake of their objective, even if they have to act immorally and harm others to achieve their goal. It's hard to create drama without portraying human transgression. The good-hearted and well-intentioned don't make for interesting characters but then who would want Macbeth as a lodger?

_____

7.   *So You Want to be a Playwright?* (2007), Tim Fountain, London: Nick Hern Books.

The role of an internal policeman is the most important one in rehabilitative work, since most people committing crime aren't banking on being caught by the external ones. Writing about the dynamics of external goal versus internal restraint is one way of getting people to address the absence of an internal cop or otherwise. It's also a great way of generating the first act of a story. For example: imagine a situation where a character changed their mind about an objective. There was a goal then an internal obstacle to achieving it. Perhaps they want to ask someone who works in their local shop out on a date but are too shy to. They approach the checkout but come away with 20 Lambert and Butler instead. Pride dented but appetite intact they then stand across the street inhaling one consolation after another, waiting in the shadows for the sales assistant to leave. You can tell it doesn't end happily.

Many lads I've worked with in prison tell me they can't think of a time when they decided not to do or say something. It's a response that's fundamental to why they are in custody and why I persist with the exercise. From what they tell me many grew up in families of uncontained emotion, self-restraint was something else that was absent in their formative years. They have also learned to hone and sharpen the practice of acute over-reaction and defence by attack, in childrens' homes, on streets and in pubs, impulsive aggression works for them — they believe they have respect because people don't mess with them. Neither do they like them or trust them.

The prison is perpetually abrasive, even in its momentary silences. Prisoners reach for violence fairly freely, towards one another and themselves, in an effort to feel something and at the same time to train themselves not to feel. Prevarication and reflection is taken as weakness — being caught off guard, as is consideration for victims. Or as one lad put it to me, *there are no victims.*

There are precious few first offence offenders in the prison, and people do not like to own up to being in custody for the first time. By the time a teenager makes it to a YOI they have generally stacked up a lot of victims. Possibly they fear that thinking in depth about one might evoke a landslide that they can't face. When I ask lads to recall a change of mind concerning the commission of a crime, they mostly cite an external factor that could result in them being caught—they spotted the CCTV or decided they couldn't trust an accomplice. As I say, there are rarely second thoughts, but then we wouldn't be working on a prison wing if there were. Often I have to settle with a hypothetical change of mind, change of heart. I get them to imagine a version of themself who thinks before he acts. The exercise is not an easy process to proscribe. It's a matter of developing the internal conflict from ambivalence to drama, from anecdote to characterization and then drawing out the writing in some way.

> I have done this before and I can do it again. I can be a kid in a candy store if I can get in that back door.... This is the house they saved up for. All that time and effort in building up possessions. Then I come and intrude on their private home. It will be very unsettling for them when their things have gone.... After the vodka wears off my conscience will kick in.
>
> *Junior*

I am told stories about walking away when confronted by potential victims, partly at least out of shame. Roy (*It's Not the Car:* see *Chapter Three*) told me he was about to steal a car off a drive when he saw a mother and baby through the window. The upshot was he decided to steal one from across the road instead, where the curtains were drawn. Our job should be to get people to write about the faces and lives they never see.

> We were in bed. I heard some shouting up our stairs. Is this a dream or a television programme? "Clare, Derek! Are you there?" How did they get in my home? I recognise those voices. "Clare, I've something to tell you—you've been burgled." My son! I go into his room and check. Then we crept downstairs dreading what we were about to find. How much had gone from our home/our living room, our place of rest, our nest egg, all that we've worked hard for. We could have been killed if we had startled them.
>
> *Glynn*

There are many examples in literature and film of a frayed conscience, and the best known character in the ultimate dilemma is Macbeth. His soliloquy at the end of the first act prior to the murder turns between rash certainty and premonitory guilt.

> If it were done when 'tis done, then 'twere well
> It were done quickly: if the assassination
> Could trammel up the consequence, and catch
> With his surcease success; that but this blow
> Might be the be-all and the end-all here, But in these cases
> We still have judgment here;
>
> He's here in double trust;
> First, as I am his kinsman and his subject,
> Strong both against the deed; then, as his host,
> Who should against his murderer shut the door,
> Not bear the knife myself. Besides, this Duncan
> Hath borne his faculties so meek, hath been
> So clear in his great office, that his virtues
> Will plead like angels, trumpet-tongued, against
> The deep damnation of his taking-off...[8]

Difficult though it may seem it is worth persevering with, possibly as I did with the support of one of the film versions. Unpick the text with a reader and then ask them to write their own soliloquy prior to an offence. The employment of Shakespeare to discuss a tawdry crime of today will be argued as a pretentious indulgence by some, but we are trying to convey to people who have acted thoughtlessly, that to be human is to think, *to stress*, and to experience self-doubt and remorse; to have a conscience that informs behaviour. Before Shakespeare, literary characters aged and angered or appeased their gods, but they didn't change much in relation to themselves. He is credited in part with *the invention of the human*[9] and there is much

---

8. *Macbeth* (I VII 1-28), William Shakespeare.
9. *Shakespeare: The Invention of the Human* (1998), Harold Bloom, London: Fourth Estate.

in his drama that relates to the lives of people in today's criminal justice system.

Exercise 33	**Motive Versus Conscience**

Ask the participant(s) to think of an occasion where they were about to commit a crime but didn't (or vice versa).

- Why did they change their mind?
- What does it tell them about themselves?
- What is or was the dominant drive?

Get them to write the monologue that portrays an internal conflict.

Discussion Suggestion 11

Why is it important to have a conscience?

Is it possible to have a conscience and commit crime?

Some of the most frustrating conversations have been when people have told me they didn't know the family they had burgled had recently lost a grandparent, or that the car they had stolen was needed to take a child to nursery, or that the victim was frightened to leave the house six months later. And if they had known they wouldn't have done it. As if there was such a thing as a convenient crime.

There is a standard offence-focused session that involves drawing a ring of impact around a crime, like ripples with the offence at the epicentre. The idea is to place everyone affected by the offence in order of proximity. You can draw up quite an ensemble cast of insurance companies and security guards, even for shoplifting, but sometimes it only serves to make the protagonist feel more empowered than they should yet no nearer empathising with anyone. In order to empathise with someone we need to know their story, their internal narrative. This is best done by meeting them face-to-face or by reading what they themselves have written about their experience. Unfortunately both of those are still relatively rare. Perhaps the exercises above can be used to augment existing work that attempts to pull back the curtain on the impact of offending on others.

Creative writing from a photograph: youth offending team.

Exercise 34   Motive Versus Trait

Ask the participant(s) to think of a character with a goal but they also have a personality trait that is standing in the way of them achieving it.

For example, the shy person who wants a date, the lover frightened of commitment, the lazy worker who wants promotion.

Ask them to write a short monologue that portrays the internal conflict.

FIRST AND LAST LINES

4

4.1   Story as Intervention

Story is how we explain who we are: our beliefs, our achievements, the injustices done to us and our transgressions against others. It is how we make our identity. Arguably we live our lives in three acts and telling tales is as innate as procreation. Perhaps the evidence of this is that the same narratives have appeared from across the continents for as far back as we know. Joseph Campbell has researched and written widely on this subject documenting the *Little Red Riding Hoods* of Peru and West Africa;[1] noting the common purpose they served as a warning to wilful daughters. Transgression is at the heart of storytelling and in my experience the opposite is also true.

The criminal justice system is rich in narrative and all sides of it are dramatised every night on television which in turn plays its part in perpetuating real and unhappy events that other writers will subsequently draw upon. The crime story has always had cachet from Kane and Abel onwards, yet my sense is that the value of reputation, of whatever quality, has risen to such stellar heights these days that some people, particularly some young people who are assailed and susceptible to celebrity culture, increasingly do stupid and harmful things merely to be able to tell the tale to peers; to a solicitor; to other inmates. Of course there are other reasons that brought them into the frame, onto page one in the first place, but it is the story of what they have done, the telling of it, that confirms their identity.

---

1.   *The Hero with a Thousand Faces* (1948), Joseph Campbell, London: Fontana Press.

> I went to get a gun from a friend who i knew would give me one to lend. There are lots of gun's in Stretford you hear about it on the news and in the papers everyday - This gun was a COLT 45 which was big and heavy Silvery black it was cold on touch and made me feel good it had 3 men in the clip. It made me feel like i was the only man on the earth. i was high with a balaclava rolled on my head it is a deadly combination

Account of an armed robbery by a teenager.

As a writer working in a prison, I've always believed my job was to get the lads to retell their real crime stories, more honestly, stripped of the mythology, perhaps as cautionary and avoidable; and to make them realise that they needed other stories to learn and to live by.

Whether you are trying to do this in a prison, a probation office or even a school, you will be working with people who are enamoured of today's popular heroes; and these are increasingly characters that always win or die trying, without qualms or a change in direction. They don't listen to the sirens or any other voices; nothing stands in their way. Few people would give Leopold Bloom the time of day in a contemporary city.

In the prison I currently work in, there is a great deal of crime memoir on the library shelves, as much again in lads' cells. The library's defence is that the genre is popular with prisoners. Add to this diet what else is absorbed in a prison, into a generally already culturally impoverished metabolism, and you might think that getting lads to write and read the narrative that challenges the criminal identity would be impossible. Not so in my experience. Perhaps the ubiquity of trash culture in prisons creates a curiosity if not an appetite for something richer than the lives of Pablo Escobar and Curtis Warren. Perhaps when you live in a world where the subversive is the mainstream, in order to carry on breaking the rules you have to look elsewhere.

The Delivery Man

Mena and Maria were sisters. Their parents had died and left them their beautiful house on the slopes of a mountain in the north of Italy. Neither of the sisters had ever been married. They loved one another and didn't feel they needed anyone else. They had promised one another they would only get married if they both could.

Mena had always cared for Maria ever since they were very young. Mena being the older and more responsible took charge over their modest grocery shop. This is where Mena first set her amazing blue eyes on the man who delivered the groceries. His name was Caesar. Six foot four and a slim toned body he would always wear his best shirt to visit the two sisters' shop. Mena used to look forward to Caesar's visits, she adored him and the feeling was mutual. Her weekends were spent looking forward to Caesar's Monday deliveries. Before each visit Mena would fix herself in the mirror, combing her hair and adjusting her make-up. She began to dress differently for work. They began to talk to one another, about music, wine, family. After many months of waiting, just as Caesar was unloading a box of strawberries, he asked Mena if she would like to go on a picnic to the mountains the following Saturday.

That night as Mena was collecting the dishes, after the evening meal, she glanced at her sister and thought about telling her the news. But the quick glance made her believe it was for the best that she kept it a secret. As Maria sewed her blouse, Mena thought her sister looked so content. The happiness was clear from the tune she hummed.

It was a sunny day; Mena stood waiting on the lane at the end of the village.

She was wearing a vibrant tomato red dress. She had a white bow in her hair. It was a breezy day and the wind carried the dress ever so slightly. Her hair followed, wandering elegantly in the wind. Driving along the track Caesar looked smart and Mena was excited to be going out with such a handsome man. The grey waistcoat, grey trousers and shiny black shoes made a picture worth taking thought Mena. Caesar told Mena how pretty she looked. Mena gave a teasing smile.

The site Caesar had picked was at the bottom of the hillside. It was hidden by apple trees and a slow moving stream cut the field in two. A few fields away Mena could see a man working his farm, ploughing his field. For a moment she wondered who he was and hoped he wouldn't come any closer. They laid out the picnic together. Caesar had brought grapes, peaches and a pear tart he had made for Mena. He pulled out some wine he had brought from his vineyard. As the afternoon moved on Mena became more and more comfortable around him and even allowed Caesar to hold her hand. They chatted about how things used to be, in a simpler time.

The journey home was slow and Mena was beginning to think about her sister. As they pulled up just away from the house, Caesar kissed Mena on the cheek, Mena just looked at him. 'I've got to go.' Mena moved quickly towards her house, without the goodbye she would have liked. When she arrived home Mena was relieved to see her sister, but hurried off to bed, leaving Maria to wonder what was wrong.

The following weekend Mena woke up to find a note on the bedside table. There was something deeply suspicious about the note; they never went shopping without each other, especially into the towns. Mena waited all day for her sister. Finding it difficult to concentrate on her work, she couldn't help but think her meeting with Caesar had something to do with Maria's sudden spurt of independence. Had she found out?

Maria arrived home late into the evening and wasn't acting herself, but when Mena quizzed her sister on what she had bought on the trip, all Maria could show was a bottle of expensive wine. That evening the sisters shared an evening supper during which they drank the bottle of wine. They both smiled.

The day at the store was long. When Mena arrived home she didn't know how to approach her sister. She arrived to find her still in bed. Knowing she would be hungry, she asked if she would like to go out for dinner.

The two sisters cycled up the track towards the vineyard. They were on a tandem with Mena steering as usual. Mena parked the bike up and then hand in hand they walked up the pathway. They stayed in silence. Mena knocked on the door. The door squeaked open. The tall, tanned figure of Caesar appeared. A great smile spread across his face and he told Mena how beautiful she looked. From the shadows Maria stepped out of the side of the stone porch. Caesar's face dropped. As he stood there speechless, a tear rolled down Maria's eye. Mena could not believe they had betrayed each other. Caesar smiled and said,

'Don't worry I have enough food for the three of us.'

The two sisters got back on the bike and never spoke of Caesar again.

Andrew

The trigger for the story was a photograph of two Edwardian women in a summer house. But Andrew chose the photo over many others, mostly contemporary images and decided to move the story to Italy; somewhere he'd never been. He was serving a long sentence and was determined to use the time to read and study as widely as was possible. He hated prison, what it was doing to him and what he had done. In the time he worked with me before he was shipped out, he never, as far as I knew, read any crime fiction or faction, nor did he ever write or discuss crime. He knew how uninteresting it mostly is. Writing was a means to escape from where he was and who he had become and I aided and abetted him as best as I could. After he was moved elsewhere he wrote to me saying how he'd learned to love reading Tom Wolfe and Raymond Carver; and Andrew's background was as averagely disadvantaged as other inmates. He was amongst a few prisoners I encountered over a period of years for whom literature was a source and an expression of transformation.

There is of course a general difference of attitude to custody by prisoners serving sentences of differing lengths. There is also, in my experience a corresponding difference in attitude to creative writing from the long-term and the short-term prisoner (I am including in the category of the long-term prisoner the ones for whom the gate has become a revolving door) and the difference is perspective. Lads serving shorter sentences are more concerned with their immediate prospects and their most recent caper; they are in general less likely to want to read or write fictional stories than the long-termer who is over familiar with his surroundings and its dog-tired fables.

It is a worthwhile challenge to encourage and support prisoners to write fiction set in unfamiliar worlds, partly because that is the *raison d'être* of fiction and partly because it creates an objective for them to live beyond the walls of the prison, their friends and family and themselves.

Exercise 35	**Far and Away (Image)**

Present the writer with a series of photographs that say little but suggest much.

The photos should be at a cultural distance from the writer: another country; race; religion; lifestyle; environment; something different to their own.

In response to the photograph ask the writer to decide:

- Where the story is set
- When the story is set
- Who is the story about; and
- How the story begins; what is the opening image; action; event; line?

It might be the great outdoors, a city overseas or something commonplace like a door; a wheelchair.

Wheelchair
photo courtesy of
Stephen Thorpe

Alhambra door.

The vast majority of offenders I have worked with are from urban areas, they have little or no direct experience of the countryside; of spending time in wide open spaces. Many express a desire to see, if not live in, a more beautiful environment which they also believe to be a solution to their offending.

The Forest

I left the city and only took with me a tent; sleeping bags; shot guns and gas hob, billycans. On the way to Canada I ran out of fuel so I stole a pick up from a cattle ranch and carried on the journey. Once in the mountains and forests I set up camp and had a rabbit I caught in a snare. In the morning I was walking through the woods and I came across a lake with a beautiful crisp shine off its surface, and there behind it, the log cabin. I went in and had a look around, it was better than the tent. No one had lived there for years. I went back to the pick-up, unloaded it and started repairing the cabin the next day...

Nathan

Exercise 36	**Far and Away (Sound)**

Play the writer(s) a selection of short pieces of music; of various genres that might not be to their taste: flamenco; classical; choral; folk; jazz. Ask them to write down:

- The emotion that the piece evokes
- An action that the music evokes — what is happening?; and
- A time and a place for the action.

It doesn't matter if the writers' suggestions seem wide of the mark, what matters is that they explore new territory.

4.2 Generating Narrative

There is a great deal written about what makes a good story or even a story at all, and anyone asking someone else to write fiction however short, in whatever form, should dip their toe into the criticism.[2] They should also endeavour to try their hand themselves. At its most basic, story has to be more than a sequence of events, more than something of a crisis.

Story is the meaning of the journey: the *why*. 'The Queen died and then the King died', are just two events. 'The Queen died and then the King died of a broken heart', is a story. We love stories. They hold us because we don't know what's coming next and in life we generally do, or think we do. It tends to be the episodes in our lives where the unexpected has occurred, the good or bad fortune that we want to write about. We say it was like a story and writing it gives it meaning. We need the meaning to reassure us of our life's purpose. We like to spend time with fictional characters that are experiencing the *good news bad news* of life and we are either envious or thankful that it's not us.

Writing any kind of story is a difficult thing to do, even for a prison or probation service anthology; it has to hold together, it has to have its own carpentry. There is always a beginning, a middle and end that needs a connection and it is worth asking, why undertake the uphill slog with people whose literacy is likely to be poor and who will struggle if not resist making it to the end?

The answer, in part, is *because* they will find it a struggle. Creative writing is the contemplative equivalent of the Outward Bound course where reaching the summit, abseiling down the quarry, supposedly builds the recidivist character. Viewing events through another's eyes, more than one pair, examining a conscience and the consequences of an action, resolving a conflict non-violently (on paper at any rate)

---

2. For example *Story; Substance, Structure, Style and the Principles of Screenwriting* (1999) Robert McKee, London: Methuen. *The Art of Compelling Fiction* (1998) Christopher Leland, Cincinnati Ohio: Story Press. *The Art of Dramatic Writing (1946)* Lajos Egri, London: Simon & Schuster.

all in well-formed sentences is a challenge. Many lads in the prison who have begun writing stories for me and with me, have bailed out before the end. But those who have completed have usually started to read fiction, and in discussion or in prose have reflected on the motives of their own behaviour in a way they hadn't done previously. It was worth the slog.

As with any exacting undertaking it can sometimes help to start with some warm-ups. The following are in common usage at drama workshops and most can be done verbally, particularly if you're working with a group.

Exercise 37   **Fortunately Unfortunately**

I left home and unfortunately it started to rain
Fortunately I had an umbrella with me

Unfortunately it wouldn't open
Fortunately the bus came

Unfortunately I had no bus fare
Fortunately someone paid for me

Unfortunately they followed me…

Exercise 38   **Go For It**

Have prepared a number of lines of invented dialogue; provocative opening lines for a story. You don't have to know the story — that's the exercise. For example:

Have you seen what they've done to Terry!?

I can't believe what I've just found…

Don't lie to me I know where you've been…

I'm prepared to stick by my beliefs no matter what…

Write the lines on folded pieces of paper or card and ask the participant(s) to choose one at random. Respond and continue improvising.

Give the participant(s) the *Fortunately* role, have fun and try to find a conclusion. There is a serious point here. The *good news bad news* element of storytelling is crucial to holding audiences and an assured tactic of soap writers and an element of our best loved stories like *Jack and the Beanstalk*. To entertain is to hold, literally; the back and forth in fortune also begs a question about where the ending will fall.

Exercise 39	**The Alphabet Story**

Improvise a story where each line begins with succeeding letters of the alphabet, spoken by each participant in turn.

At the time I saw the boy I was alone on a bridge.

Below me the river was raging.

Certain that he would drown I shouted at him…

Get to Z.

I seldom discuss with lads at the outset what makes for a good story but rather get them to develop their own and then we discuss what will make theirs better. There is a multitude of ways to get going into fiction, not least the allegory of their lives.

The memoir I'm handed is invariably voluminous, short on reflection as well as concision: the events and many are rarely themed. Admittedly to make my own work more interesting as well as theirs, and because I may not have long with a lad before he's moved to another prison, I encourage participant(s) to transmogrify their life stories into allegory. It can also serve as a means to escape habitual realism. The two below are drawn from drug-related offending.

The Glass Man

Once upon a time there was a man made of glass. He was famous where he lived. Everyone knew who he was. Most people were scared of him. The Glass Man liked this and called it respect. People feared him because with one wave of his hand he could sever them into pieces. Some children saw their reflections in him and dreamt of being like the Glass Man. But the older people didn't admire him; they could see straight through him and knew he was empty and hollow. They would recoil in horror whenever he took out his bloodstained money. Even the dogs looked away in disgust. So the Glass Man looked instead to the children. They gave him his power he thought. Then one day, one of them crept up behind him and smashed him into pieces.

Chris

The River

He lived in a small town with a big river. A was a boy with a fun loving personality with a good sense of humour. He looked up to many people but favoured his elder brother most of all. He was fascinated about what his brother and his brother's friends did. He loved the summer time and the warm weather because his brother used to go down to the river. His brother enjoyed swimming and fighting the depths. He loved what his brother was doing and wanted to give it a go even though he was told he was too young. But he mithered them time after time. In the end they gave in and let him have a swim. Because of his age the best thing was for him to start off in the shallows and work up step by step. The first few times he absolutely adored it. He'd never had a feeling like that ever. Then he started to lose interest in the shallows and started to explore other parts of the river. His brother's friends and his brother did their best never to let him until he grew up. As he tested the depths of the river he thought it was phenomenal. He started bragging to his friends about it....it became that good to him that no matter what negative suggestions was said to him he ignored them and kept exploring the beautiful blue river....

Jordan

Chris' piece came out of our first brief meeting. I asked him if he'd ever had a job and he replied: 'No. Well, only dealing drugs. But that's not a job ... is it?' His question was genuinely hopeful and not without sadness. He was 20 years old and somewhat ashamed of the answer. He described to me the contempt that people on his estate had for him and acknowledged that his income wasn't earned. None of this he told me though, was going to change his chosen occupation upon release and the discussion was fairly typical of careers interviews I have had with drug dealers. The symbol of a man made of glass was how he described people's perception of him so I suggested he write something in the style of a fairytale. Allegory can be a convenient tool sometimes. It lifts us away from the tedium of today and is meant to heighten the moral implications of the narrative. It would have been instructive if Chris's Glass Man had been faced with the shattering of other people's lives rather than his own but I doubt if he'd want to write that. Jordan's piece is an allegory about drug addiction.

> He thinks he needs the river after all the troubled times and years of going there. But he realizes that he doesn't need to constantly keep going. He searches for ways how he could possibly stop or even go once a week. He has thought about moving away but everywhere he could go will always have a river. He's thought about avoiding it

Original text from The River (see above and below).

The writing appeared to come easily to Jordan he seemed to be able to find lots of parallels. Perhaps allegory can help the writer to think about a problem or event in an altered, clearer way. But I suppose it may also serve to mask responsibility and absolve the writer from facing up to reality.

…after a few years of going regardless of what day, time, weather or company he was in, he became almost dependent on it over the years of visiting. He came so close to drowning a lot of the time, he got stuck in the tides, but still he went to the river…

Exercise 40	**Legend Has It**

Ask the participant(s) to identify a life problem: a persistent worry perhaps or a difficult relationship. Get them to describe the quality of this problem, for example: my relationship with my partner is *destructive;* I take my partner's love for *granted.*

Now animate that quality using metaphor from nature (a plant, or an animal for example) or a metaphor that is man-made (a machine, a work of art or an item of clothing for example).

The destructive relationship could be about a boy who captured a beautiful bird and put it in a cage and the bird became ill.

The love taken for granted could be about a painting bought at a car boot sale that is really a masterpiece.

The Grimm brother's fairytales are my earliest memories of learning stories. Several were familiar to me before I set foot in a school. Then at primary school in the 1960s we were taught tales and parables from the Old Testament and the stories, at least initially, were not read to us, they were told, as they had been in pre-literate Europe for centuries. One of my earliest visual memories is staring at a huge projection on a sheet pinned to a bedroom wall, my father shrouded in darkness, peering through a rattling contraption. The image is of two children facing an inhuman witch wearing a pointed hat. The children though, are unable to see the danger in front of them because they are looking at the cottage behind the witch that appeared to me, to be made of Neapolitan cake. The scene scared me and I think I left the room before anything else appeared on the sheet. Grimm's tales are charged with violence, courage and changes of fortune; cast with negligent parents; evil step-parents; the very rich and the very poor. They have always been a camouflaged method of giving good advice. Whilst some have heard of eponymous heroes, very few lads at the YOI know any of the narratives. So of late I have been telling the tales, pushing them under doors and employing them in writing exercises.

Exercise 41　　**Telling Tales**

Ask the participant(s) to read, or you can read with them one of Grimm's fairytales.[3]

Ask them to adapt the tale to a contemporary setting.

They may just tell it at first; but get them to write it.

Ask the participant(s) to think of an episode from their own life, or a true story, that they know — or we all know. Ask them to write it in the fairytale genre.

Hansel and Gretel live in London with their parents and the family are very poor. They are struggling to pay rent and Hansel and Gretel have to share a bed. Mum and dad haven't any jobs. Mum also has a mental illness and she punishes the kids but leans on her husband for support. She talks to herself at night, blames the kids for not having any money. She feels hungry all the time and the kids do nothing other than mess the house up…

Alex

4.3　　Story as Change

To me the most obvious reason why people who work with offenders should consider employing story as a tool is because story is about

---

3.　See, e.g. *Selected Tales* (2005), Jacob and Wilhelm Grimm, translated by Joyce Cruick, Oxford: Oxford University Press.

change and journey. Even if the journey is from one physical place to another, a transformation usually occurs inside the hero. Sometimes I begin by discussing with a lad stories that are familiar to us both from the perspective of how the central character changes: for example, the strap line of *Gladiator* is: *The general who became a slave who became a gladiator; Macbeth* is: *a story about a loyal subject who murders a magnanimous king to become a tyrant.* Then I might progress onto writing exercises about the how and why of character transformation.

Exercise 42   **First and Last Scenes 1**

Pick two points in a journey: a beginning and an end and then ask the participant(s) to proffer an explanation of what happened in-between. Make the beginning and the end sound improbable.

For example, in the beginning one man is swindled by his business partner then at the end he buys him a gift. Why?

The son of the injured party wreaks excessive revenge on his father's business partner and the swindled man is ashamed. He brings the victim some grapes at a hospital visit.

A man campaigns to save a threatened tree then eventually cuts it down.

The man sees the tree as a thing of beauty and when some new houses are built he saves it. But the roots of the tree cause a house to subside and he feels responsible.

Ask the participant(s) to think of a beginning and an end and then to explain the narrative in-between.

Or Alternatively

Exercise 43   **First and Last Lines 2**

Give the participant(s) the first and last line of an unwritten story. There should be a relation-ship between the lines.

He knew he could never go back home…

…he had made it home at last

I have to get off this island no matter what….

happiness is living on an island.

She knew what she had done was wrong …

at last she felt good about herself; proud of what she had achieved.

Ask the participant(s) to try and explain what occurred in-between. Ask them to come up with their own examples.

Discussion Suggestion 12

Ask the participant(s) to think of changes of attitude that they have gone through: changes in attitude to others and to offending.

How did their attitude change and why?

How do they think they may change in the future?

Many of the lads at the prison are vociferously opposed to changing their outlook or behaviour. They will do what the prison asks of them; they may even volunteer for responsibilities such as peer mentoring or serving as race equality representative; they will be known to officers as a 'good lad' and will be eligible for early release or parole but they will never tick the box of the law-abiding citizen. This is predicated on the assertion that the life strategy is working just fine. *My life's perfect* as one lad boasted to me. Jail is an acceptable and tolerable hazard for an income without working and we are challenged to propose a viable alternative. Indeed staff are subject to cross examination by prisoners about the folly of our own career choices, the naïvety of what we do. *How much do you get for this? What car do you drive?*

A lad described the shop workers he threatened in the course of robberies as *slaves*. Even if one rationalised the amoral stance, living in the shadow of custody is hardly enviable, but then all expectations have been adjusted. There's no salary, pension plan or mortgage in there, often there's no bank account or rent book. I'm now into my fifth year at the prison and see the same lads returning again and again. Occasionally I'm not even aware they've been released since the interval between has been so short. Prison is home. Before that, local authority secure accommodation was home; and before that a children's home. Home stopped being home a long time ago. Prison, prisoners say is easy. Too easy. That's the problem. If only it was harder then we wouldn't keep coming back. Then we'd change. And it is easy for many: if you can fit in, make alliances and avoid the bullying, if you know what to expect.

Trying to scare juveniles on community orders with the prospect of custody won't work. Many will thrive there. The establishment I work in doesn't feel like punishment and it could do more to rehabilitate. Young prisoners are largely contained, resting from chaotic lives, catching up with old peers and meeting new ones and everyone inside the gates is waiting for time to tick by. Some lads do find the experience dreadful. They may be vulnerable or the ethic is alien to them and they had careers in motion on the out. Some will harm themselves.

I know that many lads desire a *normal life*, a family and a nine to five job, yet feel that the quest is futile. The encroaching economic climate will chill many of us to our bones, and people with dozens of convictions and several sentences know they will have to compete with graduates to wait on tables. Increasing numbers of employers want criminal record checks and available social housing is fast becoming a curiosity. Many offenders see no point in joining a queue for six pounds fifty an hour and will not endure the poverty and humiliation bestowed by living off the dole. As one lad put it to me after umpteen knock-backs: 'I can't even see the point in being polite anymore'.

In the late-1990s I worked in an open prison as an employment worker and found a lot of employers refreshingly open to giving people a second chance. Out of the 200 prisoners I worked with, 60 were offered work on release. That was when Manchester's regeneration was beginning to bubble and the hotel and restaurant kitchens needed unskilled labour. All those jobs everywhere are now taken and criminality, drug-dealing in particular is viewed as a safer financial bet. It is the equivalent, the actuality in fact, of thousands of businesses all over the country; many seemingly small three generation family businesses.

I've had the logistics of life on the streets explained to me many times but an image that has always stuck with me is of teenage boys from Liverpool balancing my diary on their fingers, tilting it back and forth and arguing about its weight in kilograms.

There are also prisoners and would be ex-offenders endeavouring to do what many, including their own probation officers see as the impossible; get a job, start another life somewhere else, start again. It is the road less travelled, like a scene in an adventure film or a series such as 'Lost' where one or two individuals embark on an intrepid rescue mission against all the odds. They have to be admired, foolhardy though they may be. Some do make it through the pass, but my time spent working at the prison has impressed upon me how socially divided Britain has become from the country I grew up in. Not merely in terms of income, but in a way that is more serious more injurious. It is about the enormous distances in ambition, outlook and morality, between those brought up with books and foreign languages and musical instruments and those brought up with violence and cash.

There is a widening cultural divide in British society that has nothing to do with immigration; in fact it has expanded itself most noticeably into the cracks of white British society. The continuing privatisation of further and higher education and the decimation of adult education mean there is less scope to beat the odds. There is a sadness about the prison and it comes from the sense that lives are limited inside and outside the institution.

Some practitioners argue that if one is working with people that either can't or won't join in society then there is little point in asking them to write as an intervention. It is assumed they must work their way up the hierarchy of needs and more functional priorities like housing, or drug addiction must be addressed first. But inadvertently excluding people from the arts only compounds their poverty; it is also the case that tailoring the arts for the socially excluded (whoever they may be) runs the risk of emphasising the apartness of the participants.

A difficulty I had with many interventions when I was a YOT officer is that they were presented as an appeal to the self-interest of the young offender. *Anger and violence isn't working for you—you need to stop, think, act and reflect before you get into trouble again.* Anger and violence do work well on the level the perpetrator intends a lot of the time. Sure, some relationships might be in crisis but differences are unequivocally resolved. In my experience people who are persistently violent do not regret the assaults and brawls. Their lives would be emptier without them. Young men in prison will tell you that they do in fact stop, think, act and reflect before and after armed robberies and burglaries. They're just not doing it as well as they'd like to. Offenders generally do have an abundance of needs; typically they nearly always lack consideration for other people, and the reasons for this (not least British society's aggressive individualism) are beyond our reach.

The criminal justice system is awash with talk of targets and skills offenders must learn whilst the most important lesson has to be the unquantifiable thing called compassion, and compassion almost as an act of duty. If carried out assiduously writing becomes such an act, as does every form of art. One is giving part of oneself to a stranger, unconditionally, who may in turn not give you house room. This is why some prisoners I work with are reluctant to have their work published in anthologies. A lad even once began his memoir:

> Here is my story. Anyone who wants to read it is welcome to, but if you don't want to then you can fuck off.

Not exactly inviting the reader in. Many young men in Britain these days, inside and outside jails, are so armoured against injury they get their revenge in first and in doing so their own sensibilities are stillborn. Writing honestly requires people to lay down their armour.

4.4   Story as Premise

We expect there to be a premise in story as much as we do in our lives. We will often recommend a book or a film by its theme: the central idea. Of course stories aren't always written with a premise in mind. The writer may begin with a character or a situation, but usually by the end I suspect they are sure of the message it conveys.

There has been recently, particularly in film-making, a trend towards the decidedly 'no message' narrative, for example *Pulp Fiction*. I still maintain that audience expectation is being second guessed and then subverted and, whilst there are memorable scenes, the most memorable stories do more than entertain. As a story can be said to have three acts, every premise can be said to have three parts.

An example of a premise might be: *Honesty overcomes dishonesty* or *Jealousy leads to loneliness.* The first is either a cause of or in conflict with the third part. We know from our premise what drives our protagonist and we know how it concludes. The most familiar stories to us usually have an identifiable premise and as a way to introduce the idea to the participant(s) it is worth distilling a story or two to its basic ingredients. For example:

Romeo and Juliet: Love conquers hate and death.

Titanic: Love conquers wealth and death.

Carlito's Way: A man's past will destroy his future.

Discussion Suggestion 13

Ask the participant(s) to think of a proposition that they have experience of or hold to be true: *Loyalty always comes at a price,* etc. Get them to elaborate and illustrate the statement; to tell you the story.

Alternatively, ask the participant(s) to think of a significant experience from which a lesson was learned.

As the tutor, come up with a proposition of your own and likewise elaborate by example. Why is this true for you?

Discuss why one person might hold one thing to be true and another the opposite, for example, *One should never inform on a friend; friendship is more important than money.*

Can one ever stick to such principles and why is it important to believe in them?

Exercise 44	**You and Your Big Ideas**

With the participant(s) write a list of four propositions each.

- Are there any that you both/all agree on?
- Choose one and with the participant(s) construct a plot that illustrates it.

For example, if you were to choose *Loyalty always comes at a price;* a conceivable plot could be about someone who covers for his employer's mistakes only to be blamed when the company is investigated.

Ask the participant(s) to write the story in no more than four hundred words.

If one is writing a story with a premise in mind then you have to at least envisage believing in the premise.

The participant(s) may or may not be able to write the story but the process opens up a discussion about values in a way that isn't a form of cross-examination.

4.5   Story as Conflict

Story can also be viewed from the perspective of one kind of conflict or another. There is always conflict in story however sub-textual. *Protagonist* derives from the word combatant and *drama* is Greek for deed, or action. No struggle equals no drama equals no story. Stories are about winning or losing, by overcoming obstacles or ignoring advice. We want to see if the hero will do whatever they have set their mind to. Either way they must go through hell and high water along the way.

Stories are a laboratory where we test the character; put him or her under extreme pressure to see what they are made of. So what kind of different laboratories are there? Here are five varieties.

An individual versus self

The celibate priest who falls in love; the doctor who can't decide whether to treat a terrorist or not; the spouse who considers an affair.

An individual versus another individual

The priest who falls in love with a married woman; the doctor and his superior; a husband who wrongly accuses his wife of an affair.

An individual versus a group

The strike breaker who needs to pay for his son's medical care; the young footballer who comes out as gay and is ostracised; the politician who disagrees with his or her party.

An individual versus society

The priest who has no believers; the doctor in favour of euthanasia; the young girl who is an illegal immigrant.

An individual versus a situation

The priest and the earthquake; the doctor at the car crash; the shopkeeper during the riot.

Discussion Suggestion 14

Ask the participant(s) to describe when they have experienced conflict under any of the above; from either side.

How did it feel to be beleaguered or faced with someone who wouldn't fit in? Ask them to describe their point of view; to ascribe the other side's point of view. What would they say?

Exercise 45	**Write What You Don't Know**

Ask the participant(s) to describe an *individual versus self* conflict and to write the differing points of view as if they were two distinct voices.

Ask the participant(s) to choose an individual scenario they wouldn't automatically identify with and to write a monologue for that voice.

I just found out. That she knew all along. Alicia knew my dark, shameful secret. She knew my secret and took it to the grave with her. And I couldn't tell. We were married fifteen years and I couldn't tell. She seemed to love me as much, even more after, as when we were first married. She was faithful. Not like me. And now this day, a year after I buried her... a letter arrives. The letter's from Jane, Alicia's sister. At first, I couldn't bring myself to read it, but eventually, I read it... over and over again. The letter stuck in my head like ink to paper. Alicia knew about my secret. But why did she not confront me about it? Why did she not shout at me, or leave me, or show even a bit of emotion? How could she even bring herself to look at me after what I had done? Yet she stuck by my side, loved me, cared for me, as if nothing was wrong. I could never forgive myself for what I had done, but did Alicia forgive me? How could she? I had lied to her for two years. For two years I had an affair with Jane, her own sister! Yet Alicia knew and carried on as if everything was all right. Why?

Fifteen-year-old girl on a Community Penalty

4.6   Action and Consequences

The award winning film 'Crash' (2004) connects a number of seemingly unrelated characters through chance, enmity and goodwill. Paradoxically it is their racial and social divisions that unite the characters in the plot. Another way of approaching story is to select seemingly random images or objects and devise a thread to join them in a narrative. Admittedly there is a similarity here to the First and Last Lines exercise, earlier in this chapter, but I think it requires the imagination to work harder. Take three photographs or objects for a beginning middle and an end and present them to the participant(s).

Lightbulb courtesy of Stephen Thorpe. The other two photographs are by the author.

Don't dwell too long on the objects: a dice; pizza; a cricket ball. The key thing is that at least one of the connections in the narrative needs to be unintended, pure chance. For example: Jim suggests to Tony they go to a casino and they both lose money but Jim borrows money from Tony for the last unsuccessful throw of the dice. By way of repayment Jim suggest he treats his friend to a pizza afterwards.

The next day Tony has food poisoning and is off work. He lies on the sofa tossing a cricket ball and accidentally breaks a mirror. Whilst trying to clear up the mess he cuts his hand and the dog also walks on the glass and cuts its paw. He's lost a day's pay and can't afford to take the dog to the vet. He's in the doghouse at home now as well because his partner believes he has a hangover. There's a row. Tony blames Jim. He goes to see him. This is just the beginning, unintended or otherwise, of a mounting dispute.

There are all sorts of home-made tools you can employ to trigger story events. I have my own plot necklace, a series of small objects on leather chord: a ring, a nail, some jade, a dolphin, a coin, etc. The participant(s) can start wherever they like but must follow the sequence.

I have some picture cards which I use to prompt three acts of a story. Using cards to read personalities or anything else, even in jest, is to be avoided and almost certainly proscribed in custody anyway. Superstition and providence is big in jail. It determines whether people are arrested, the sentence dished out and the chances of parole. Lads take the God pill overnight and conspiracy theories about everything from 9/11 to the jury with the unanimous verdict circulate at will. I also have some mock tarot cards which I use to prompt three acts of a story.

Someone takes a voyage that leads to wealth. But also the destruction of something else. Copyright www.psycards.com Illustrator Maggie Kneen.

A stranger arrives and affects peace in a hitherto fractious
community. But also unleashes the beast in someone.

There is a refrain amongst offenders that futures are controlled
by others, in or out of jail. At the same time they will claim that
they are doing just as they please. It is telling how many lads find
prison an acceptable if not a preferable place to live. A place where
you can't open a door, or hear yourself think; have a shower or make
a brief phone call without the permission of an officer; a place of
perpetual uniformity. *Everything is done for me here*, as if that were
an enviable circumstance. But crime can be an expression of plain
laziness, not just in its commission but more so in its mind-set.
Unemployment is certain to spike crime statistics because of the
poverty it bestows but also because of the debilitating inertia and
powerlessness it leaves people with.

When I worked in youth justice the trinity of offence-focused
work was antecedents, behaviour and consequences. Narratively, we
can substitute anticipation, event and aftermath. Stories are about
hypothetical actions and consequences, intended and otherwise and
the exercises above, as well as taking the participant(s)'s imagination circuit training, ought to be a vehicle to reflect upon their own
actions and consequences.

Ask the participant(s) to think of an action of theirs that has had unintended positive consequences for others and ask, 'Could you rightly take credit for that?'

Likewise, when there were negative consequences for others. If the impact is unintentional, 'Are you still to blame?'

Can they think of a time when they themselves were the victim of the unintended consequences of someone else's actions?

4.7   Narrative that Reveals and Conceals

There is some prisoners' writing that patently lacks emotional literacy. What is also significant is that in discussion they appear to not desire it: they always seek to obfuscate the search. A discernible pattern in the writing of young men who have been convicted of sexual offences against children is that it is always far into the camp of fantasy fiction, not surprisingly violent fantasy fiction. Characters are always furnished with special powers, protagonists are part human part creature/demon transmogrifying from page to page, meeting to meeting, leaving me off balance and ill at ease. The authors are also generally unwilling to take direction about their work, the world which they have created.

Working with people who have sexually offended against children is a highly specialist field and I am not qualified to comment indepth upon it. I have though in the course of my career worked with a sufficient number to recognise the trait of relatively voluminous writing with precious little human characterization. My approach on the advice of NOMS and psychologists has always been to make people, actual people, the subject of the writing starting with them.

Story can be used with offenders and those at risk to discuss and examine the cause and effect of behaviour and its moral purpose. Remarks about the media's influence on criminal behaviour is usually met with accusations of censoriousness but frequently young men tell me they'd threatened a cashier in a particular way because they'd seen it in a film. The film isn't the reason why they committed the armed robbery but imitation becomes part of the goal.

I have listened to thousands of stories of crimes over the last 15 years, by both victims and offenders, some minor, some as serious as one can imagine and very early on it became clear to me that often behind the motive of money or violence lay the motive of power for people who were otherwise powerless. In a story we have control of events, and the audience. In my experience many offenders, particularly young men, feel and behave as if they are caught up in some exciting and dangerous narrative of which they are the hero. The other people in the frame are unimportant bit players. Story should be considered as a means of intervention, if for no other reason than distinguishing fact from fiction.

PAST AND FUTURE SCENES   5

5.1   Writing Drama as Intervention

Drama has been a productive writing form for me in the prison. This is partly because I enjoy writing plays, partly also because there seems to me something instinctive about offenders and drama. Maybe it's all the acerbic dialogue in their lives. Maybe it's because they are less likely to have read a novel than seen a film. They believe at the outset that this is a shorter way to tell a story, a story that can be told through speech, in a vocabulary they are familiar with. There is more to it than that though. Drama is by and large about action and event—deeds. Actors need something to do not just something to say: an objective. A major part of the narrative takes place in the external life of the character, which is where offenders and people at risk often perceive their problems to be.

It can be said that we are all always playing one role or another but with offenders this is arguably more the case. It is a part that many have worked hard at learning. Prison is a kind of theatre; the wing a stage in the round with a balcony and fine acoustics; everyone has a costume, a theatrical walk on set and all the lads and officers project extremely well.

Augusto Boal has explored in depth how 'theatre can… be the repetitive acts of our everyday lives'[1] and for sure there is an offender characterization that people at risk need to learn to become the risk itself. Contact with police and solicitors as a juvenile, appearances in front of a bench of magistrates will school people in storytelling

---

1. *Games for Actors and Non- Actors* (1992), Augusto Boal, p.11, London: Routledge.

(developing a good backstory to one's offence is an essential part of mitigation).

There was for a time an ironic apothegm recited by Liverpool lads at the jail about why they were there: 'Me ma didn't love me boss'. It's a satirical strapline about pre-sentence reports and years of dialogue with social workers. The role wherever you are has its own idiom, subversive in its fluidity. It also has its own non-verbal language and that isn't diplomatic either.

The part occupied by the outlaw has always enlisted cultural accoutrements for support, of late an industry has developed from which you can download: music; film; television; memoir and fiction. The identity and personality of offender as a character is ever enlarging. There are many facets to familiarise oneself with, for example, there is a particular kind of masculinity in evidence in the jail, more easily defined by what it doesn't defer to; a sort of masculine fundamentalism. It is unequivocal in its opinions, in how it feels; it doesn't do nuance or self-deprecation. It seeks to dominate.

The misogynistic lingua franca for women (*bitch, bird, ho*) repeatedly goes unchallenged and it is not possible for some women workers or visitors, to walk around the concourse without suffering sexualised invectives from windows. Many lads will refuse to read their work out publicly or even have their name attached to it, as they feel any overt indications of intelligence and tenderness will mark them down as *gay* or a *muppet* or a *woman* and thus a candidate for bullying.

When I listen to young men in prison talk about their relationships with women they invariably describe a battle, a sexual feud in which they must have the upper hand. But then they see almost all social relationships as a contest and consequently they're nearly all in crisis. It is alarming how many lads I come across in the jail who are serving long sentences for serious crimes arising from arbitrary disputes: remarks made by a neighbour; a stranger in a pub or a corner shop—interpreted as an attack on their exalted yet susceptible self-image.

I've met many lads who have lost employment and otherwise good prospects, because they became engulfed in a vortex of escalating conflict that emerged from very little. The risk factor is all in the outlook.

> My family has been in a feud with another family for the past three years and it is still on-going. This feud started a few years ago when this family had an argument with my family. It has carried on due to the fight for respect and to have the upper hand. I am now in prison due to this as I set their family home on fire to scare them from messing with my family. The feud is still not over. They currently have the upper hand due to getting me sent to jail.

> *Tom*

Daily life for some lads, in and out of jail, is a war; they refer to one another as soldiers. Those of us who believe that progress can be made through cooperation, whose opening stance to others is mutual respect and approachability, are only the misguided in need of enlightenment.

> When I meet a bloke who I don't know, I want to know who they are and whether they are a dickhead or not. I need to know where people stand in the ranks. You have you and your boys that you trust — your army. You have people who don't want to be involved and just stand aside and you have the enemy — the people you are against, just like in a real war. This is nothing to do with crime. Conflict has made me who I am. Fighting lets me know I am alive.

> *Tom*

It is also the case that without an emotionally deprived upbringing one cannot convincingly play the role. Many lads at the YOI who are otherwise inexpressive, manage to articulate a backstory of emotional scars effectively.

I don't like letting people in. If I let people in I get close to them, then they either let you down, or disappear. Whenever I get close to somebody, whenever I get settled, start coming into my own, I get moved on, have to start all over again. They throw me back into a lake, like a fish they've hooked, but don't want. I keep everyone at arm's length, don't show any weaknesses to play on. This is much better. Nobody can play with your emotions. If you don't let them affect you, if you don't get caught. I've been in so many homes, instead of waiting for the inevitable I decided to run away, be within walking distance of my estranged family, to swim freely, and not to take the bait. Being bad is honest. It's not a lie. You're bad no matter who it affects. Being good is just a way to prove you're normal, when everyone has flaws. What is the point in being good? What does it mean to be good? To think about other peoples' feelings, concerns, opinions. The word is consideration. It's like walking on dry land. It just doesn't feel right.

'Arms Length' by Lee

5.2   Dramatic Lives

Up to a point the people I'm writing about can write better dialogue than anything else. Better dialogue than many writers. Up to a point. It's about as authentic as it gets and it's frequently abrasively funny. Characterization too can be terrific. The aphorism *write about what you know* is both apposite and cautionary in the case of offenders. Whatever tactics are employed — photographs, foreign objects, exotic music or my pseudo analysis of their dreams, the scripts, at least the first ones, often cast back to something extraordinary that happened, some juncture that determined their future. A recurring narrative is that of one teenage boy leading another astray: the salad days of trouble, 'green in judgement, cold in blood'.[2]

---

2.   *Anthony and Cleopatra* (1.V.73), William Shakespeare. 'My salad days/When I was green in judgement, cold in blood'.

Mates[3]

Scene One

Somewhere in Liverpool.

Monk early teens, rides across the set on a BMX bike. He is approached by Mark.

Mark	Gimmie a go of your bike.
Monk	No.
Mark	Why?
Monk	Me ma won't let me.
Mark	What diya mean 'Me ma won't let me?' Yer ma's not here. It's only me and you.
Monk	Yeah but…
Mark	Yeah but nothing lad. Gimmie a go on yer bike or I'll punch you in the face.

Monk gets off the bike, Mark takes it.

Monk	Are you gonna give me it back?

Mark laughs and cycles in a circle around Monk

Monk	Right you've had a go, give it us back now….Come on…

Enter Chopper.

Chopper	Yer alright lad?
Monk	He's acting like a tit. He took me bike.
Chopper	Did he? Give him the bike.
Mark	What's it got to do with you?
Chopper	He's me mate.

---

3. *Mates,* a 20 minute piece, won a Koestler award in 2009. It was performed to an invited audience as a script in hand at the Royal Festival Hall along with two other pieces from English prisons by Synergy Theatre Company in the same year.

Mark	No he's not.
Chopper	Well he fuckin is now. So leave him alone.
Mark	You know what. I was gonna punch him. But now I'm gonna punch you.

Mark gets off the bike, squares up to Chopper, punches him. Chopper goes down. Mark turns his back on Chopper who gets up and punches Mark in the back of the neck, knocks him to the floor and kicks him, he is about to stamp on Mark's head when…

Monk	Don't!
Chopper	Why?
Monk	Got me bike back haven't I?

Chopper kicks Mark one more time, walks away

Monk	You're Chopper aren't yer?
Chopper	Yeah. What's your name?
Monk	Monk.
Chopper	Yeah I've seen you around. (Mark limps off) What yer doin now?
Monk	Goin home.
Chopper	Shall we have a sit off? Kill some pigeons? (Chopper takes his catapult out)
Monk	Don't mind.
Chopper	I hate muppets like that. (Chopper kills a pigeon) Yes!
Monk	Why yer doin that?
Chopper	Cos it's fun. Killing pigeons is fun. Something to do. Do'ya wanna smash some windows instead, get chased?
Monk	No we'll do this.
Chopper	Where d'ya live?
Monk	With me mum and dad. Where do you live?
Chopper	In a flat. With me ma. Bet your home's all nice.
Monk	You don't know that.
Chopper	Don't I? Here have a go.

Chopper gives Monk the catapult. Monk fires at a pigeon and misses

Chopper   That was a shit shot that. Here!

*Chopper takes the catapult back and executes the pigeon at close range. He gives it
back to Monk who tries again and misses*

Chopper   You missed on purpose!
Monk   I never. Just a bad shot that's all.
Chopper   Come on we'll go and smash some windows.
Monk   I have to go home and have me tea now.
Chopper   Forget yer tea. We'll go and rob some chips, tell yer ma to fuck off.
Monk   I don't talk to me mum like that. Doesn't your mum make your tea?
Chopper   No she's always sick my ma.
Monk   What's wrong with her?
Chopper   Doesn't matter. (Monk gets up to go) See yer Tomorrow then?
Monk   Yeah, alright.

Eddie

In Scene Two (which is not reproduced here) Monk emerges from
a police station to tell Chopper he wants nothing more to do with
him. Chopper says this is because '… you think you're better than
me, because you come from a proper family… an cos me mum's
on the gear n that.' When I asked Eddie what happens next, he
shoved a biscuit into his mouth, held up his splayed hand and said
five years later. The portrayal of this pair in their 20s is well drawn,
they're the same people but older. But he found it a lot harder to
write because he was 16 with a patchy education and he hadn't lived
the remainder of the script.

Often the first two scenes or so are drawn from experience, the
rest they need more help with. Many won't finish. I labour against
that but have to accept it. Prisoners have to be harried into endings
and second drafts of anything. Crime is about pursing short cuts,
chasing maximum reward through minimum effort. Violence is also
a short cut: the quickest way to superiority. Art asks for the maximum degree of effort and gives no certainty of any reward. Art is

the opposite of crime. That is why, for rehabilitative purposes, it is important that offenders are introduced to it.

Some lads are incredulous that there isn't always a prize for their writing, no remuneration or certificate. It's one reason I insist they do it. It doesn't work alongside an exaggerated sense of entitlement. Others are grateful that they have completed something for its own sake as if each piece served as an act of atonement.

What happens in these mini dramas beyond the autobiographical is where the work about action and consequences is to be done. To begin with, the job is to get people writing in the form. Start with something that comes easily.

Exercise 46   Making a Scene (Plot)

Ask the participant(s) to describe a dramatic event from their own life. It can be an ordinary dramatic event.

Get them to write down some dialogue and character profiles.

They should be asking themselves: What does this character want and what's standing in their way?

Now ask them to fictionalise it in some way. Create a fictional character; a fictional place and time; a fictional ingredient to the scene.

| Exercise 47 | **Making a Scene (Character)** |

Ask the participant(s) to think of two people that they know, but who don't know each other and wouldn't get along either.

Put them together in a scene — where they are forced to co-operate.

For example; they have to work together; they are both lost; are strangers in a foreign country.

They both begin to influence each other's behaviour — Get the participant(s) to write this.

Below is an extract of what two lads came up with for the above exercise. The only other guideline I gave them was that it mustn't be set in a jail cell.

The Berth

Yasmin is in a cabin on a boat reading a law book when Emily stumbles in…

Emily Hiya! I take it you're my room-mate.

Yasmin Erm no, I'm in a single berth. You must have the wrong room.

Emily Well the cabin crew told me this is my berth and I'm sharing with someone.

Yasmin Well you must have the numbers mixed up because I booked a single. You need to go and double check with them.

Emily You must be nuts. I'm not walking all them flights of steps with these bags.

Yasmin Then use the lift.

Emily Don't like lifts me. Do you want some of this vodka?

Yasmin No. I want to study in my berth

Emily Oh what yer studying? I'm a student me.

| Yasmin | I'm studying law. I want to be a police officer. What are you studying? |
| Emily | Things like alcohol awareness. I want to help people me. |

J and K

Making a Scene (The World)

Ask the participant(s) about a place they have been that has made an impression upon them.

They must imagine that they live there now and always have done.

A stranger appears (from where the participant(s) *actually* live now) there is conflict between the two characters.

Write the scene.

Discussion Suggestion 16

How do other people influence you?

Why is it important to cooperate with people who you don't get along with?

Would you be different as a person if you lived somewhere else?

5.3   Over the Bridge

Assume then we have two characters in a crisis together who really don't get along or an outsider arriving to disrupt the stability of a haven. We might have an inciting incident but where is the story going; what is the premise of the drama? Playwright Alan Plater described writing drama as like leading people across a foggy bridge where only the writer knows what awaits on the other side. For some, attempting the labyrinthine task has to be done by careful design. The plot is constructed for the characters that become the story and not a line of dialogue is written until we are sure how the final scene will end. For others the process can be at the organic end of the spectrum and everything begins with an enigmatic line, an arresting image imploring the writer to follow their instincts. The premise, the meaning, will find its way to the surface.

For me the two most useful books on playwrighting are: *The Art of Dramatic Writing* by Lajos Egri[4] and *The Crafty Art of Playmaking* by Alan Ayckbourn.[5] They are clear and concise guides on the carpentry, but if one is working with the uninitiated, and for reasons other than the art itself, the discipline is best regarded as a set of tools rather than rules.

The most straightforward advice I can offer is to give your characters a desire and then enjoy thwarting it: *put them up a tree and throw stones at them.* At the beginning of the drama we have to find something they want, and then to begin to prevent them achieving it at every turn to see how they react.

'Eddie's Kitchen' is a 20 minute piece written by two lads about the challenge of *not* being a drug dealer. It was borne of my appeal for them to morally justify their occupation and defend the harm that they were inflicting on the community by pushing drugs. Both argued that they never had to *push* anything, actually the community wouldn't leave them alone; demand far outweighed supply and selling drugs for a living was not abnormal, nor was it denounced by those around them, rather it was welcomed as a much needed service in the area. It was a job that was difficult to leave.

One lad said that his kitchen had become in effect a shop front and he was glad to have a break from work now he was in prison. We talked about who used to come to his kitchen and even I was

---

4. *The Art of Dramatic Writing* (1946), Lajos, Egri, London: Simon & Schuster.
5. *The Crafty Art of Playmaking* (2002), Alan Ayckbourn, London: Faber & Faber.

surprised. I asked them to write the opening scene; the harassed drug dealer who would rather be doing anything else. Here's an extract from the result:

Eddie's Kitchen

Scene One

A kitchen in a council house; somewhere in Liverpool.

Eddie walks around his kitchen, phone to his ear.

Eddie No no Yan—I'm running dry mate…. I could do with it before Friday… I'm not joking.

Ends the call but it immediately starts to ring again

Eddie Hello…. How much? An ounce? …. Okay….can't it wait til tomorrow? … Aren't you supposed to be in court today? … Well how are you gonna defend someone when you're stoned? You're not better at it when you've had a smoke—I should know—I was in the dock for shoplifting and you got up and said I had nothing to do with the kidnapping….

Now there is a knock at the door. Eddie runs to the window to see who it is. It's Tom

Eddie Hold on a minute Gary, someone at the door.

He opens the door to Tom, a university lecturer

Eddie Can you just fuck off for half an hour?
Tom I need to come in Eddie, please.
Eddie Ten minutes and I want you out.

Tom comes into the kitchen, Eddie's back on the phone to Gary

Eddie	Look Gary you come and then you're gone… Okay… five minutes. What can I do yer for Tom?
Tom	You're not gonna believe this Eddie.
Eddie	I've got a feeling that I might.
Tom	She's gone and left me.
Eddie	Yeah I know Tom, you already told me.
Tom	When?
Eddie	Told me ages ago that your wife left yer.
Tom	Not me wife!
Eddie	So who's left yer now?
Tom	I do wish you'd listen a bit more Eddie. Naomi. Naomi's left me.
Eddie	Ahh that student of yours. Do you not think she was a bit young for you?
Tom	Final year next year.
Eddie	Right. Fair enough. So. How much do you want?
Tom	Almost a mature student.
Eddie	I haven't really got time for this today.
Tom	I'll have a half….no tell yer what, make it an ounce.

Eddie fetches him a bag

Eddie	Don't smoke it all at once. One and half ton that.
Tom	Do you take plastic?
Eddie	Do you take a fuckin kicking?
Tom	Can I pay you tomorrow? You know I will Eddie.

Eddie takes some out of the bag

Eddie	Look just take that and clear off.

As Tom is leaving Gareth the solicitor arrives at the door. Tom lets him in

Gareth	Is he in?
Tom	In the kitchen.

Gareth enters the kitchen

Gareth	Yes Eddie my man
Eddie	How much yer after Gareth?
Gareth	Enough to get me through the afternoon. In front of that Judge Nicholls this afternoon.
Eddie	Is he a bastard?
Gareth	Out to get me.
Eddie	Yer reckon?
Gareth	Yeh they all are. I'll need some of that skunk I had the other week. Worked a treat that did.
Eddie	Yeah?
Gareth	Oh aye got this lad away with two years.
Eddie	Parking offence was it? Er this came by me last week. From Afghanistan.
Gareth	Can't have been easy.
Eddie	Part of the war effort.
Gareth	You're a hero Eddie.
Eddie	Here's one that I made earlier.

Lights a spliff gives it to Gareth — who takes a drag

Gareth	Ohh yeh. It's gonna be a not guilty I can tell.
Eddie	What did he do?
Gareth	You know I can't even remember now.
Eddie	What was that thing you were telling me the other day… the secret to a good…
Gareth	To a good defence?
Eddie	That's the one.
Gareth	The secret to a good defence is to make the criminal….
Eddie	…look like a victim. But how do you do that?
Gareth	Law school. Make him look like a victim of mistaken identity, a victim defending himself, a victim of poverty… of a bad upbringing. Trick is to get people feeling sorry for the person who's broke the law.
Eddie	And what's that thing called again…
Gareth	What?
Eddie	That you have to do….
Gareth	Articles. You writing a biography of me or something?

Eddie	No one would believe it would they? Right, time to go Gareth, I've gotta meet someone.

Gareth exits.

The real Eddie had even worse customer service by all accounts and told me he hated the fact that everyone from university lecturers to BT workers would sit in his kitchen and tell him their troubles. He wanted their money not their company. The Eddie of the play wants the money but he also wants something else: Claire (below). Of course he can't have both because Claire wouldn't approve of his occupation. In Scene Two below, Eddie makes use of his customer knowledge by telling Claire he does something else for a living. It's standard for drug dealers to have a front occupation, the lads came to the plot idea very easily and had no trouble writing the scene.

Scene Two

Claire and Eddie, a street at night

Eddie	Did you like the film?
Claire	Not bad.
Eddie	You should've said you didn't like it. We could've walked out done something else.
Claire	I didn't mean it like that. Thanks for paying by the way. And for the meal as well.
Eddie	It's OK. Not short of a few bob me. What shall we do now?
Claire	Not sure. You've not told me what you do yet?
Eddie	Me? Well, I'm solicitor. Training to be a solicitor. Doin me articles.
Claire	Oh really? Which courts do you work in?
Eddie	Oh all over me.
Claire	You'll probably know my dad then.
Eddie	Why, he's not been in trouble has he?

Claire	No he's a magistrate.
Eddie	Oh I see.
Claire	I'll ask him if he knows you shall I?
Eddie	Expect he sees lots of different solicitors.
Claire	Bound to remember you though. I bet if you two got together you'd never stop talking. Why don't you come round for Sunday dinner?
Eddie	Can't, busy I think. Look Claire, I'm going to have to go.

Eddie's desire to win Claire is obstructed by his drug dealing, so he lies, invents another occupation. It's complicated as well because it's his drug dealing that allows him to date and treat Claire in the first place. Just by referencing the above we can see a way to begin a drama.

Exercise 49   What's Cooking?

From the exercises in *Chapter Two* ask the participant(s) to develop a character with a desire; like Eddie a desire for a relationship.

However, the character perceives an obstacle to the desire being fulfilled and the obstacle is in their own life. It could be their status or wealth, their family background, a health problem, something in their past, a current relationship, etc.

Ask the participant(s) to write a scene where the central character covers up the problem from the person they want to be with.

Discussion Suggestion 17

Have you ever had to keep things secret in a relationship? Lied about your past?

How would you feel if someone who you were in a relationship with was keeping something about them hidden?

How has committing offences affected your relationships?

Realising that the solicitor lie is going nowhere, Eddie tells Claire that he must come clean and explain that he is in fact a university student—another complication he knows he can't sustain.

Claire	A student!
Eddie	Is that alright?
Claire	Course.
Eddie	I thought you might think that was a daft thing to do.
Claire	No way I was a student myself
Eddie	Really?
Claire	Yeah, wished I hadn't given it up now.
Eddie	What happened?
Claire	I had this hopeless teacher. Always trying to get off with his students, always looked like he was stoned as well. You might know him…

Exercise 50 — It's Complicated

Covering up the truth in the previous exercise somehow makes matters worse for the character. They have dug themselves a hole and feel they must get themselves out of it. Whatever they do though — just makes matters worse.

Ask the participant(s) to come up with a scenario or devise one with them and ask them to write the scene.

In the end Eddie drives his customers out of the kitchen and tells them he is shutting up shop. It's the only way he can invite Claire round to the house.

Claire	So I finally get to see where you live
Eddie	I'm sorry I haven't invited you round before. I had a few people staying.
Claire	Nice kitchen. What's that smell?
Eddie	What smell?
Claire	Have you been cutting the grass?
Eddie	Yeah, I've been cutting a lot of grass recently.
Claire	So what's this essay you've got to do?
Eddie	Oh the essay. Look Claire, I need to tell you something.
Claire	Again?
Eddie	I'm not what I said I was. I'm not a student either.
Claire	I did have my suspicions Eddie. So what actually do you do?
Eddie	Well I don't really do anything.
Claire	You're on the dole?
Eddie	I've not got round to that yet.
Claire	So what have you been doing?
Eddie	I'm not sure. I'm just chilling I guess.
Claire	So what do you do for money?
Eddie	I haven't worked that out yet.
Claire	Eddie, this doesn't look very good. You're doing nothing, going nowhere with no money.
Eddie	I'm gonna change all that Claire.
Claire	So you say but you tell me lies.
Eddie	Claire, honestly, this is the real Eddie.
Claire	Really?
Eddie	Yeah
Claire	Well he seems like a right time waster to me. And I don't waste my time.
Eddie	Claire, wait!

Discussion Suggestion 18

Life can be easier being dishonest sometimes. Why?

Do you wish you were more honest?

Think of a time when you paid a price for being honest. Is it better to be honest even if you're worse off as a result?

Exercise 51   **Coming Clean**

Does the character tell the person they want to be with the hidden truth?

Does the other person find out? Then what happens?

Ask the participant(s) to write the scene.

Of course Eddie goes back to dealing from his kitchen and the lad's point was however self-justifying, well made. The piece is no more than 15 minutes long though the writing process took weeks. The three of us would sit and talk about the story and the ramifications of drug dealing. The writing in the session was done by each lad taking a character and improvising. If it sounded right, it was written down. Then I would give them homework to do on the wing which was, at best, erratically undertaken. The next day we polished and continued.

It is true that neither lad would have written any drama without me; yet both lads did go on to write independently afterwards. They were not trying to become writers, but rather writing creatively about their own lives, possibly to resolve or rationalise things. The story, dialogue and world of 'Eddie's Kitchen' are theirs not mine. My input was in helping them structure the piece and then editing it. But that's what a writer in residence is for.

'Eddie's Kitchen' was performed in the chapel as part of a showcase of prisoner's work. The cast was made up of the two lads and three actors from a local theatre. I shredded some green papier-mâché for Eddie's drugs and he used a blackboard rubber for a phone. Often what diminishes short dramas written in this context is their episodic nature. Whenever I have written or devised drama with people new to writing there tends to be too many short scenes in numerous locations, borne I guess from watching the odd soap. No sooner does the tension rise in a scene than we have left it.

As a suggested reference point for some writing, I asked a group of lads to watch a particular film that was on Film 4 for a week. *The Hide* (2008)[6] is set entirely in a Suffolk bird hide, it takes place in real time and has only two characters. On the face of it, it doesn't sound like a film that exploits the medium but the claustrophobic effect helps build the tension towards a cleverly executed denouement. It is a writer's film that employs a unity of time and space just as *High Noon* (1952) does where we watch the clock run down for Gary Cooper in a small western town.

The following week I set a number of lads the task of writing pieces like the aforementioned: operating in real time and in the same location. Three pieces were written, one set in a taxi; one set on a street and one set in a prison library. All three pieces eventually produced had the theme that crops up daily as an aside in discussions and no doubt on courses run by psychology departments. This is the theme of moral equivalence; that those in authority are not necessarily morally superior to those in prison. The comparison is mostly made with politicians, lawyers and the police.

The moral code of the offender is not a system; it's not even a code. For many there is little that's taboo beyond the omerta, yet when the MPs expenses scandal made the news there was an outbreak of

---

6. *The Hide* (2008), was the debut film of director Marek Losey; based on the stage play *The Sociable Plover* by Tim Whitnall, who also wrote the screenplay.

comparison and self-justification on the wings. The reaction was naïve and hypocritical, but also slightly reassuring that people were at least morally resentful about something. I pointed out to a Salford lad that Hazel Blears hadn't actually brandished any weapons, but still he wanted to stand his ground next to or above his Member of Parliament.

Prisoners are always comparing and contrasting their deeds to other prisoners and anyone else who is officially castigated. The assertion is an invitation to debate and challenge. It's also a lever that can be pulled one way or another.

Damage Control is one of the short real time pieces about a disgraced politician (Tom James) visiting the prison to request a prisoner to use his outside contacts to 'deal with' the journalist who had revealed the extra-marital affair. Naturally he is offered something in return.

Tom	I expect you know someone who can help me Laine.
Laine	Help you in what way?
Tom	Cure me of this revenge.
Laine	You must be joking. Don't you politicians have enough blood on your hands, sending soldiers off to fight your wars?
Tom	Come on Laine, wars have been happening since the start of time, whether it's over money, religion, oil, we've all got our own agendas. I've got mine.
Laine	Look at this. A public school boy Oxford graduate with a house in the country for playing golf at the weekend and he's talking murder.
Tom	I just want him frightened that's all. The way I've been frightened. Why does my career, my family, my life have to be destroyed because of one little mistake?
Laine	Her? The boyfriend?

Laine is presented with a dilemma by Tom, a choice between two undesirable alternatives: either to help the politician by committing an illegal act and to secure a private education for his son, or to refuse the offer and deny his son the chance to follow in his father's footsteps (and possibly worse). It's far-fetched but it held an audience on stage and on prison radio for around 15 minutes. Again the scenario flatters the prisoner by denigrating the representative of authority but it was and is the beginning of much discussion about moral reasoning.

Asking people to write out their own fictional dilemmas can be a more challenging and revealing task than posing questions and scenarios from an offence-focused manual.

Exercise 52	**Sticky Wicket # 1**

Ask the participant(s) to create a character and place them in a situation where they are asked to do something that they know is wrong for the sake of their family.

For example, a child is instructed to provide an alibi for a parent. They must at least resist the pressure put upon them.

- Write or improvise the scene.
- Examine and express both sides of the argument.
- Develop the story.
- What are the consequences either way?

Exercise 53 **Sticky Wicket # 2**

Ask the participant(s) to create a character and place them in a situation where they are asked to do something that they know is wrong in the context of work.

They must at least resist or initially refuse, for example they might be asked to dump something illegally. Perhaps they agree and then inform on the company.

- Write or devise a scene.
- Examine and express both sides of the argument as well as the conscience of the central character.
- Develop the story.

Exercise 54 **Sticky Wicket # 3**

Ask the participant(s) to create a character and place them in a situation where they are asked to do something by peers that they know to be wrong. They are reluctant to act, but they don't want to jeopardise the friendship.

- What are they asked to do and what do they actually do?
- Write or improvise the scene.
- Develop the story.

Example

Chad	What period you got now?
Tom	I don't care. Not as if I'll be listening.
Chad	I think you're in IT Room twelve.
Tom	What are you in?

Chad	I'm with Mr Ainsworth, history. Love it, been in top set since year eight.
Tom	On your back you! Come on the bus and trek to me Nan's. Got to get her some shopping, her arthritis is getting bad
Chad	I need to go to history
Tom	Come on, me Nan loves you. It'll make her day.
Chad	We'll go after school
Tom	The home help will be there then. And she said she'd give us a few quid if we did her shopping.

Two: the street

Tom	Eh look there's a Poundland. Let's go and rob some munch.
Chad	I thought we were going to your Nan's
Tom	We'll rob some hair-curlers for her
Chad	What will she want with them?
Tom	Dunno. I just wanna rob something
Chad	Why?
Tom	It's something to do ... come on.

Glynn

Discussion Suggestion 19

Have you ever felt compelled to do something you knew was wrong?

Why didn't you refuse?

If you had refused, what would the consequences have been to yourself; to others?

Exercise 55   **What's My Motivation?**

Ask the participant(s) to go back to that time when they felt compelled to do something that they knew was wrong.

•   Ask them to find a motivation to refuse.

•   Write the scene.

5.4   A Word about Dialogue

For our purposes we can take dialogue to be anything that comes out of a character's mouth. It is an artificial construct and not the same as speech. Rather it is (in part) designed to give the reader essential information about our characters, our stories, themes and their background and context. It is a conduit for emotions.

Dialogue is a practicable way to get people writing, particularly if they lack confidence, because most people start off attempting to write naturalistic dialogue: dialogue that is meant to sound like real speech. Some offenders, if writing dialogue in their own context, can do so very authentically and that is a hook worth using.

As I have already explained, the vocabulary and how it is spoken is a fundamental component of the offender role, a rejection of society's norms, more so than the clothes and the walk, second only to the commission of crime. There is perhaps an exponential relationship between the measure of someone's estrangement from the law and the drift of their voice towards the impenetrable. Some of the most refractory lads in the YOI from Manchester will proffer as few sullen words as possible whilst conversely the Liverpool lads are belligerently garrulous. Both seem to strangle words at birth and all risk incurring a self-inflicted speech impediment in pursuit of the ghetto talk.

There are differing vernaculars even from within cities and whilst everyone filches from black America, British underground colloquial speech is thriving and evolving faster than management jargon. It is a way of expressing locale, attitude and sometimes an ugly masculinity.

Over the last decade or more I have gradually become bilingual in urban slang and whilst I swear more than I realise (swearing isn't swearing in a jail) I avoid making concessions to slang whilst working with offenders. I say this because I have heard many in the industry attempt to engage young offenders by dipping into the jargon, as if vocabulary alone can build rapport. It's patronising, embarrassing and never works and anyway the objective here surely, is to get the people we are working with to operate successfully in another vernacular. That said, to begin with we should get the people we are working with to write dialogue in a voice that they know well, a voice that they are expert in and can revel in. They will enjoy seeing their spoken voice recorded on paper, typed up even, it will get them writing and nothing breathes life into character more quickly than convincing dialogue.

Uncle is a private landlord

Uncle	Yer fitting in well son. Keep up the good work and you could be going up a step.
Chopper	I'm ready for the next step.
Uncle	Think so? Here's a little extra cashish lad. Want some beak?
Chopper	Sound.

Uncle passes Chopper a package.

Uncle	You've done alright this first month, I'm gonna trust you with a couple of properties that are a bit special. I want you to look after them.
Chopper	Sound.
Uncle	Is that all you ever say lad? Aren't you gonna ask me what's special about them?

Chopper	No.
Uncle	Well I'm gonna tell yer, you need to know.
Chopper	Right, sound.
Uncle	Stan lives at one of em.
Chopper	Stan?
Uncle	Stan is an ol' fella and there's nowt special about him. He lives downstairs at number ten. Upstairs is where we keep what I've just given yer. You have to look after the upstairs. I've a few young lads who do the weighing and bagging. Watch em cos they're dodgy. Now you're gonna need some equipment, know what I mean?
Chopper	Scales like?
Uncle	A piece Chopper. Know anything about pieces?
Chopper	Oh aye loads. Let me have a forty five.
Uncle	You've been watching too much telly lad. Start you off on a nice nine millimetre.
Chopper	Sound.
Uncle	You know what I like about you? Yer thick. Too thick to stitch me up.
Chopper	I've more respect for you than that.
Uncle	Yeah and the other thing I like about you, is you're game as fuck.
Chopper	I'd never grass on no one.
Uncle	That's what I wanted to hear. Next question. How can we get rid of that muppet Monk?

From 'Mates' by Eddie

Eddie told me that in his early teens he used to bag and weigh heroin for a landlord in the upstairs of a tenancy. To get across what it was like I suggested he wrote some drama based on it. The above is not particularly colloquial but it does feel authentic and it emerged very easily on our first and second meeting. If I'd asked him to write poetry or prose about it I doubt if he would have, and it may well have been further away from the reality. If you are working with someone for the first time, consider beginning by asking them to write dialogue to tell you something about themselves.

Exercise 56	**Lend Me Your Ear**

Ask the participant(s) to write a page of dialogue between two or three people set in their own area.

The participant(s) can be one of the characters. It could be a conversation in a shop, a bus or a pub.

For the purposes of this exercise, it doesn't matter what the dialogue is about but rather that it sounds like real speech.

Asking people to write dialogue in the voices of people of very different backgrounds to their own, can serve as a useful perspective exercise.

Exercise 57	**Lend Me Your Voice**

Ask the participant(s) to repeat the above discussion, but amongst people from different: social backgrounds; ages; gender; cultural backgrounds.

An awareness of what characterises real speech is one essential of being able to write dialogue. In informal situations it is usually rambling, often inconsequential, it does not proceed logically and people don't respond to one another but rather they talk about several subjects in the same conversation. Real speech is often very boring. In order to make dialogue naturalistic it needs to incorporate some of the former, except, obviously, the last.

What is most interesting about dialogue, naturalistic or heightened, is what isn't said; what lies between and behind the lines: the interpretation and intent. This is where the thinking and the drama is. We often talk about *reading between the lines* as a way of understanding the truth of what has been said or written. Philip Priestly and James McGuire's[7] cognitive programme for offenders *Stop Think Act Reflect* identifies communication skills as one of the three common deficits (along with poor problem-solving and moral reasoning) present in people who offend. In training people to read others we train them to appreciate how they themselves are read. Many offenders will tell you they don't care and see their indifference as a virtue. Many others though are unconscious of how they come across and some might even want to tune in.

Exercise 58	**Behind the Lines (Dialogue)**

Select a page of dialogue to look at with the participant(s).

It might be something that you are both familiar with from a well-known film or play, or something written by someone else you are working with.

Write the hidden meaning of each line.

Example

The Listener is a short piece that was written for the Prison Radio station. It concerns the Listener Scheme where selected prisoners are trained to be confidential listeners available round the clock for other prisoners to talk through problems. I should say that the dialogue is probably not representative of how an encounter would work in reality; after all, it's a play. (Lines in bold are my suggestions for subtext).

---

7. James McGuire, University of Liverpool. McGuire is recognised as an international expert on what works in reducing reoffending. His publications include *Understanding Psychology and Crime* (2004), Milton Keynes: Open University Press.

The Listener

Prison door opening

Rob   Boss boss can I see a listener?

Off   Okay. Give me a minute son.

Door closing, another door opening

Rob   Are you available for a call out?

'It's the middle of the night. Do you really want to do this?'

Ryan   At this time? Yeah, sure.

Door opening

Ryan   What's up? What's up lad? You asked to see me.

Rob   You got any burn?

'I need some company.'

Ryan   I'm not here to sort burn out for you. If you wanna talk then I'm here to listen.

'I'm not here for that and you're not the first person to do this.'

Rob   If you've got some skinny burn I'll sort you out on Friday.

'I really don't know where to start.'

Ryan   I'm gonna get off now. It's late.

Rob   Wait. Hang on a sec. You won't tell anyone what I tell you will you?

'I'm vulnerable.'

Ryan	Look mate everything you tell me is confidential.
Rob	Sure about that?
Ryan	It stays with me. All I do is write down what time I came in here and what time I leave. And your name if you don't mind.
Rob	Forget it. I'm not telling you my name. I'll tell you everything else but not my name.

'But I'm not that vulnerable that I can't make light of this.'

Ryan	Why am I here?
Rob	It's about my mum.
Ryan	What about her?

By Daniel

One way to identify subtext is to define each line as a transitive verb. Specifically what is the line attempting to do to the person to whom it is addressed?

Example

Rob	Okay. Look I never get to see my son. I haven't seen him in about two years. All because of an argument I had with the mother of my baby. My mum gets to see him every single weekend and when the weekend comes I just feel like I'm being pushed aside. I feel like my mum should let me see him if only for an hour. I've put this to her but she doesn't take me on.

Confiding

Ryan	Do you want to repair this relationship?

Reassuring

Rob	Obviously yeh; I've tried to. They say I'll never change.

Imploring—'take my side.'

Ryan   And will you?

Probing

Ask the participant(s) to come up with transitive verbs from hereon.

Rob	When I get out of this lifestyle I'm living.
Ryan	And how are you going to do that?
Rob	You need to start telling me something about you.
Ryan	Why?
Rob	You should know, you're a listener. What's your name?
Ryan	Ryan. What's yours?
Rob	Robinson
Ryan	Is that your first or last name?
Rob	It's me name.
Ryan	So how are you going to get out of this lifestyle?
Rob	By moving away to Northampton with my dad.
Ryan	Oh brilliant. Why don't we all move to Northampton with your dad?
Rob	Who do you think yer are, yer clever bastard?

The novelist Russ Litten[8] donated to me two enjoyable exercises around dialogue and subtext that he uses in writing workshops.

---

8.   *Scream If You Want to go Faster* (2011) Russ Litten, London: Heinemann.

Exercise 59   The Mattress

A man and a woman walk into a department store and buy a bed. They have some unspoken problem between them; it can be financial, emotional, practical, whatever, anything you like, as long it's personal and deeply felt. They are approached by a salesman, who engages them in conversation.

Ask the participant(s) to write a conversation where the salesman and the man and woman only talk about the bed.

The reader must get a sense of what the hidden problem is by the dialogue.

Exercise 60   The Telephone Conversation

Ask a participant(s) to write down one side of an overheard phone conversation.

They have to invent a situation where one person may be calling another and adopt the character of the person who phoned up and leave gaps for what they imagine the other person is saying.

Say to write no less than a dozen lines.

Pass the paper over to the next person and get them to fill in the missing dialogue.

We rarely say exactly what we are thinking and we often ascribe our own meanings to what is said to us. Offenders and people at risk are often poor at subtext in both directions. Some see a threat where none is intended and react as such even before anything has been said. It comes partly from being nurtured in emotionally volatile homes, from harsh and erratic parenting that has trained them to be hyper-defensive; partly also perhaps from a competitive society that values winning and wealth at all costs and often commends aggressive behaviour.[9]

Discussion Suggestion 20

Do you sometimes misinterpret the subtext of what other people are saying?

Describe an occasion where you might have done that?

Dialogue is an excellent vehicle to explore victim awareness, even where the offender has never met or seen the victim. I asked a lad who was in custody for a number of burglaries to imagine that he was observed in the act by holograms of the people who lived there. Holograms that, though they were unable to stop him, demanded a dialogue with their burglar.

Before a line of dialogue is written though, we needed to set the scene by envisaging who lived there through a detailed recollection of the environment. I asked him to describe the exterior and interior of the house and determine the ages and occupations of the people who lived there. Then he had to describe his hologram physically, giving him or her an emotional life and a name; as much character work as if they were creating a fully fleshed-out work of fiction.

Excerpt

David   They said my alarm would go off if someone did that.

---

9. Visiting speakers from celebrity chefs to ex-footballers besiege YOIs offering guidance and wisdom to inmates. Many of them are invited in for lucrative fees on the assumption that prisoners will listen to them because they've appeared on television. They have included a former contestant from the avaricious world of *The Apprentice*.

Brian	Not if you cut the power. Now shut up.
David	Don't tell me to shut up in my own house. What are you doing?
Brian	What does it look like I'm doing?
David	How can you behave like this?
Brian	I don't think about that stuff. I need money, can't get a job, this is the only way. Stop asking me questions….

The lad said it was the most difficult thing he'd been asked to do as part of his sentence. When he wrote a fairy story for his niece he did so prolifically and fluently, he was also an avid reader, but when he tried to write the scene above he really struggled. I took this to be a good sign. I have spoken to a lot of young men about a lot of burglaries and my sense is that they often envisage the absent occupants to a degree, possibly out of guilt or curiosity or even satisfaction. Entering into an imaginary dialogue can be a good basis for a restorative justice intervention.

Exercise 61   **Who Wasn't There?**

Ask the participant(s) to describe in detail, a house or premises they have burgled.

Ask them to envisage who lived or worked there and to create at least one realistic character.

Then to write the scene where they were burgling the property in conversation with the victim who is demanding that they justify what they are doing.

Discussion Suggestion 21

With regard to the offence above, ask the participant(s) what they imagine the victim or victims remember most about the burglary.

Exercise 62	Aftermath

With regard to the above burglary or another the participant can recall, ask them to write two pages of dialogue between victim family members the night after the burglary.

If it is an individual, then assume close friends or family members visit.

5.5   A Word about Monologue

Monologue like dialogue is dramatic language. It is meant to be heard, performed and, if we are reading it to ourselves, to be imagined as spoken. It is the voices of characters in action and, although they may be talking about a past event, it is what they are experiencing in the present that concerns us. A monologue is a mini play really, using one voice. It is like an operatic aria when the emotion of a character's subtext becomes overwhelming. Because there is only one voice doesn't mean there is only one character. The monologue may be addressed to the audience or reader, or it may be addressed to someone else, in the character's life. When it is done well then by the time we get to the final line we know more about the character than the character does.

Looking again at the monologue in *Chapter Two*, Of George and Spain, the piece is written in the form of a diary which helps to plot the change in psychology. Emotionally it engenders pathos but then has the uncomfortable twist for us at the end. Scott was on a six month order to me when I was a YOT officer, much more a lad at risk than a risk per se. He spent five weeks on this piece, an hour a time, I merely asked him questions. I felt it was a good use of his appointments.

We'd been over his offence repeatedly, now he was given a goal, problems to solve and required to empathise with someone vulnerable, and he had a reason to turn up other than the threat of breach proceedings.

The shorter word count in monologues can belie a great deal of character and narrative work that isn't immediately obvious on the page. In dramatic writing, the 'point of attack' as they say, is not the beginning of the story. Unlike novels, drama does not have time to begin at the beginning. They tend to begin just before a conflict erupts out of the history of the story you are telling. Dramatists talk about the importance of jeopardy in a story: the question of what is at stake.

Scott has his character staking everything on a dream that we know from the second line isn't going to materialise. We know it before the character does and then we watch his dream evaporate. The crisis leaves him sitting on his bed with a loaded gun. The theme of self-deception is always worth exploring with someone who is in denial about their own behaviour.

How then can we employ monologues to work specifically with offenders and people at risk? Most obviously we can ask people to write their mind-set during the commission of a crime or to try to give their victim a voice.

…It's done, over with. I leave through the fire door. October, the look of a cold day. I stash the bag down a run-down alley, no CCTV down here. Then, Darren told me to go back to the bingo hall this way, where there *is* CCTV. I told you it was a job worth doing. We were having breakfast three weeks ago, in my caravan, Darren dunking his biscuit in his tea. Outside caravans into the distance, trees beyond them bending in the wind, cars on the motorway zooming by. *Make sure you get an alibi* said Darren, *go to a shop where there's CCTV. Timing is everything CJ.* We didn't plan for Paul, he wasn't supposed to be there, but I dealt with him brilliantly. Now I polish it off with an alibi. At a shop I buy a bottle of water, conversation about her day. *Have you been busy? Quiet today. Normally like that on a Friday.* The bottle of water costs 89p. So I give her a twenty pound note, take it back, then a ten pound note, then a five pound note, *oh wait, here's a pound.* When you annoy people they remember you. This is how you get an alibi. I make my way back to the bingo hall to report for work. I've done it haven't I? The perfect crime. I'm gonna get away with this, aren't I?

Colin

We were in bed. Then the neighbours woke us, shouting up our stairs, like a dream or a television programme. *Claire, Derek, are you there?* How did they get in my home? *Claire, I've something to tell you, you've been burgled.* We get up and we creep down stairs dreading what we are about to embark on. Someone has been roaming around our living room, our place of rest, our nest egg, all we have worked hard for. If one of us had got up for a drink we could have been killed…

Glynn

A more demanding approach is to set the task of a multi-voice. The piece below includes a son, his mother and the victim of the son's offence.

Who is He?

Christopher has been getting ready for his new job. What a lovely job he has got for himself. He will be great with the guests, it's been so hard for him to get a job. But does he really have the job? That's what I'm worried about. He says he does but I've seen no proof. Maybe he won't show me because he wants me to trust him. Trust, that's a funny word. I bet he ends up going out tonight.

"Mum can I have the internet dongle please?" I'm always asking for it. She should just let me keep it in my room. Mind you she doesn't trust me so that will never happen. What she doesn't know is I've stopped taking my anti-depressants. She doesn't know that I'm doing fine. She will see one day I'm fine and doing well on my own. I make a phone call. "Hello Nats, what yer doing tonight?" I ask this question after I've decided I'm staying in and going to bed. I don't know this yet but the question is the death penalty of my freedom.

I knew he'd go out. He's too predictable. I'll be sleeping with one eye open tonight. What's the odds he's arrested this time? Two to one probably. At least he's with Natalie. I feel he'll be okay with her. She's trustworthy, but who's paying? Who's got the money like? When I drink, I drink to my limits. Not Christopher.

Another night beside my mother's bed in a hospital. I wonder if she'll leave this time? If my mother is sent home, how will I keep my job? She needs constant care. I can't do that and I don't know how much longer I can do this. I've been up since 6 am and I've got to get up at 6 am again today. Two am now, how am I going to do it? Why can't my brother do it? It's his duty as a son. Mind you he's always been selfish as a son.

Who says I can't drive? I can drive this. It's just a twisty start. I know this from when I was a kid. Stagecoach had an open day and they taught me how to start it. It's a lovely noise, the fumes coming out of the exhaust as the engine ticks over. The whole thing is vibrating into life as I press the accelerator to the floor. They shouldn't've kicked me out of that nightclub. I can still taste the aniseed sambuka flowing down my throat, lager just for starters, the music is still in my head on this bus. 3.30 am dark like sleep. Everything is rushing by like time travel. I've written my own highway code for the night and I'm not about to make that roundabout at this speed so that car will just have to move. If I hit it, I hit it....

Why don't social services do more? They should because I need my job. I have a family to feed as well. Going to need a bigger car to carry my mum every-where. I hope....sshtt a bus!

I'm doing psychology now. I want to know how the mind works. I don't know how my own mind works. As soon as Nat's had said "I'll buy the drinks", that was it, my mind changed. I've got to use the time in here well. My little sister doesn't want to talk to me anymore.

Chris

> I Woman Before!
>
> Another night beside my mothers bed in hospital. I wonder if she'll leave this time. if my mother is sent home, how will i keep my job because she need's constant care. She cant do that and i dont know how much longer i can do this. Ive been up since 6 and ive got to get up at 6am today. it's 2am now, how am i going to do it. why me, why cant my brother do it. it's his duty as a son. mind you hes always been selfish.//
>
> II Woman After
>
> Why dont Social Services do more? They should because I need my job i have a family to feed aswell. Im going to need a bigger car to carry my mum everywhere with the family because this one is too small. Oh i hope she's...ooooh SHT! Bus!

I also use monologue as memoir by asking lads to go back to the point in their past that they feel set them on the path to offending.

I am eleven. I am in the kitchen. The kitchen is full of men, the women are not allowed in here because of our culture. There are many conversations going on at the same time. A mixture of Scottish and Irish accents. I am in a corner drinking a can of Guinness in a daze. There are two men in front of me talking about my father's childhood and the mischief they got up to. They are the same age as my father and I'm just sitting here expecting him to walk into the kitchen. Walk in with his long grey hair tied back in a pony-tail with his jeans and vest on and his tattoos on show from his bulging muscles. People respected him, he was a fighter. It is sinking in that he is never going to walk in again. I have got to go and see him. I stand up and go into the living room. The coffin is shining there are big gold handles on the side of it. I look at my father lying there, pale. He doesn't look like my father at all. His face is drip white. The men come into the room and start to speak to my father like he is still alive. They say…

Joe

> I am Eleven. Am in the Kitchen. the Kitchen is full ov men. The women arnt allowed in here Because ov my culture. There are many conversations at the same time. there is a mixture of Irish and Scottish accents. i am in a corner drinking a can of Guiness in a daze. There are two men in front of me talking about my fathers childhood and the midlife they got up to. They are the same age as my father and i'm just sitting here expecting him

Part of the original draft of 'I Am Eleven' by Joe.

5.6 About Improvisation and Performance

I have used improvisation to write drama far more in mainstream youth theatre than I have in prison. On a practical point it's not as easy as one would think to get a chosen group of prisoners in the right room at the same time. 'Good' prisoners are very busy people. They are in demand in workshops, education, in cleaning the wing, on offence-focused courses, at meetings as representatives of their peers. You can rehearse a prisoner for weeks to play a couple of scenes as Banquo to find that on the day he has an unannounced legal visit or he's been shipped out to another prison — or in my case he's decided to hide in the waste management department rather than perform.

The other reason is to do with practice. The ceiling of inhibition tends to be lower with lads in the YOI than with children who have chosen to join a youth theatre. Prison isn't always a safe environment to risk looking ridiculous in a drama game and many lads lack the self-confidence to act in front of their peers. But again, the obstacles are the very reasons for the endeavour and over the last five years I have rehearsed lads alongside professional actors on texts written by prisoners and plays written by William Shakespeare, John Steinbeck and others. All performances I have organized at the prison have been a mix of writing by prisoners and something off the shelf. Significantly it was at the suggestion of two lads that we took on scenes from *Othello* and *Macbeth*; both had come across them at school.

Otherwise, it is not as difficult to generate interest in Shakespeare in a prison as one might think. London Shakespeare Workout has been doing it for many years.[10] The general attitude is, it's a given that this is good but it's also in another language that nobody in here understands—which is the very thing one must exploit. If time isn't taken to unpeel the text then its beauty will be missed (appreciation of beauty is an important part of rehabilitation). The text also carries people who can't act, which is most of us. The room has to concentrate on the words that address our human flaws as potently as any literature we have. It's also pleasing to hear different accents working on an unfamiliar language; as long as the diction is good enough. Accents are unfettered in prisons, as are opinions. It's one of the few places you can have an honest conversation these days.

When prisoners are writing drama for me we will sometimes improvise in the most basic way. I may get people on their feet and ask them to stand or walk like their character and I'll interrogate them until we find something worth writing down. I might even go as far as both of us, or the whole group if there is one, writing lines on pieces of paper that are folded and put into a hat to be chosen at random and responded to. But I do not generally ask people to devise drama through a process of games or workshops though I can see its value. That approach is another discipline and another text book: *The Geese Theatre Handbook*.[11] When running sessions on a pre-release course I ask lads to think of behaviour in terms of roles that can be practiced and played.

---

10. http://www.londonshakespeare.org.uk
11. *The Geese Theatre Handbook* (2002) Baim, Brookes and Mountford (eds.), Hook: Waterside Press

Exercise 63   **As You Like It**

Ask the participant(s) to think of their current behaviour as a role in terms of vocabulary, tone of voice and body language.

- Ask them to describe their vocabulary, tone of voice and body language, from someone else's point of view.
- Are they coming across as they intend?
- When have they consciously or unconsciously behaved differently — played another role?
- How were they different then?

Ask the participant(s) to demonstrate with you or another participant in a role play.

- What roles will they play in the future? Again demonstrate.

Discussion Suggestion 22

Does how you behave depend upon who you are with?

What are the different roles you have played in the last week?

Should people behave just as they like or are there rules?

Performance isn't only about acting; it can be about reading and reciting. This also requires preparation and a degree of nerve. I have known a lad vomit before reading a short poem to an audience in the chapel. Performed readings in a prison can contribute to undermining the pro-criminal culture; to establishing a cultural strategy that promotes a more generous ethic.

Articulate expressions of empathy by hardened young men to an audience of peers throws down a gauntlet you can see and feel in the room. Performance should also be part of YOT work, probation services and pupil referral units. It is good practice for participants to read aloud or perform other people's work, it is good practice for staff to read their own and beneficial for the people you are working with to learn how to be a respectful member of an audience.

I write plays with offenders because I am often working with groups of difficult young men and if we're all involved in the same drama then it brings the whole room into the same scene at the same time. I get offenders to write plays because I want them to see and feel how other people might react under pressure; that other people might choose to contain their emotions; might choose not to fight, unleash or say anything at all, might not have a choice but to sit upon how they feel and tough it out between the lines. I get them to write plays because it is a creative rather than a destructive act that develops intelligence, sensibility and literacy and because I (possibly naïvely) hope that on release these young men will think about going into a theatre.

There is a great deal of talk in criminal justice circles about offenders suffering from low self-esteem. Many do. They come from poor families ridiculed by consumerism. Many are ashamed to talk about their parents. Their families don't match up to any glossy media representations other than in social documentaries and tabloid stereotyping. They know they are in want but can't quite put their finger on it.

I just wanted that shiny new motorbike he had worked for. He had everything and I had nothing. I was jealous of his life. I couldn't see my life being like that. I felt like he was laughing at me. I had nothing to look forward to: no job; family problems. Every single day I saw his wife climb into his car. He spoke to me once; called me 'a waste of time'. I felt like the lowest of the low, the bottom of the pile. When I look back at what I've done I regret doing it. It wasn't just the bike. It was the anger inside of me. A lot of bad things happened to me as a kid. A lot of violence. A lot of crime around me. Crimes that involved lengthy sentences. I started joining in with it when I was eleven. Burgling when I was thirteen. It made me angry because I wanted a good upbringing. A normal one. With no violence. To live a good life like my mates had. I was jealous. I wanted what they had. I was jealous of everything. I need to make my life a better life.

Ed

Writer and psychologist Oliver James does articulate the relationship between inequality and violence in Britain, most notably in *Juvenile Violence in a Winner-loser Culture.*[12] Between 1979 and 1981 the proportion of boys being raised in low income families rose from 19% to 30% and has more or less stayed at that figure ever since. James argues that this fact is inextricably linked to a rise in violence and that there is a direct relationship between inequality in developed societies and higher levels of crime.

Individual young men in prison talk to me about the motives for what they do but not necessarily the causes; though they are nearly all from poor backgrounds. In general they see our society as a severe place and believe everyone's actions to be motivated by money or a self-interest of some other variety. They are a hostile band of brothers; casualties of the winner loser culture yet at the same time its greatest proponents, many possessing excessively high self-esteem: *Do you know who I am...who you are dealing with?* makes its way from television screen to inmate, from window to window. When an exaggerated sense of self encounters a colourless humdrum life, the fall out, the subsequent vent of fury, can make for a crisis resulting in harm and incarceration.

Either way, what they do have to deal with is a lack of potency in their lives. Few of the lads I work with have experienced meaningful achievement. They seek to acquire something for nothing (a facet of celebrity culture fast destroying ambition) and even when they

---

12. *Juvenile Violence in a Winner-loser Culture: Socio-economic and Familial Origins of the Rise of Violence Against the Person* (1995), James, Oliver, London: Free Association Books.

do, in fact when any of us acquire something for nothing, we know deep down it is worth nothing. In the absence of the ability to be potent, so the argument proceeds, some will strive for omnipotence, and in doing so they will persecute others who are more vulnerable.[13]

In teaching young men in prison to read and write passably, in getting them into the habit of writing for the purposes of investigation and pleasure, they may acquire a little potency; they may acquire a different kind of esteem. It's not that they have too much or too little self-esteem, but that their self-esteem is based on the wrong things.

Exercise 64	Power and its Uses

Ask the participant(s) to recall or envisage a scene where they felt powerless and people with power over them misused it.

Get them to write the scene including stage directions.

Conversely ask the participant(s) to write a scene where they themselves have misused power over someone else. It may or may not have been during an offence.

Discussion Suggestion 23

Ask the participant(s) how it felt to be in each role.

How should power be used?

Get them to give you an example of how they would use it fairly if they could.

13. 'Potency, Impotency and Omnipotence' from a paper by David Millar, Honorary Senior Lecturer in the Centre for Psychoanalytic Studies, University of Essex. The paper: 'Just Youth: The Denigration, Denial and Dignity of Youth Offending, A Psychoanalytic Contribution to the Debate on Delinquency' was delivered at the Nacro Youth Crime Conference. of 2010.

WHAT POETRY CAN DO

6

There is a lot of poetry in prisons, and not necessarily in the library. There is a lot of poetry everywhere these days and some of it isn't poetry. Lads at my own YOI write poetry for their mothers and girl-friends, for the prison anthologies and sometimes for each other.

If you want to explore writing with offenders and people at risk then you have the advantage, and the disadvantage that they may have already written poetry. Even if they haven't, people are gener-ally prepared to try poetry more than any other form of writing. It is arguably the most undertaken of all art forms. From a pragmatic point of view poetry has the advantage of usually having fewer words than prose or drama and is assumed to take less time to write, though this is by no means the case. Lads I work with often want to have a poem discovered and finished in one session and usually it is. It has the advantage of being suitable to read to receptive audiences but the disadvantage of being seen solely as a means of catharsis, and by many of the people, particularly young people I have worked with, as always requiring rhyme.

For the most part lads at the YOI begin writing poetry with me and then if they want to write again it's as likely to be prose or drama. To make progress poetry requires a degree of technical proficiency that one labours at, it requires returning to the text repeatedly and it requires the writer to read poetry, as much of it as they can. My experience has been, over years of writing poetry with offenders and people at risk, that like the rest of us they discover that writing poetry that people want to read is harder than it seems. But of course, as I have said elsewhere, we are not expecting to turn prisoners into poets, poetry lovers possibly; more so we want to know how poetry can be used as part of the practice that changes people.

People in prison and elsewhere will write poetry whether they are asked to or not, and they can enjoy poetry and crime equally, I have wondered at times if one feeds the other, and for those reasons alone writers and education workers with offenders and people at risk need to intervene with the form.

When I first came to the jail there were plenty of graduates from my YOT caseload to work with, but to find new punters I held a poetry competition for the major occasion of Valentine's Day.

My Girl Whitley

I love you Whitley I swear I do
I'm sorting my head out
I'm doing it for you
Being without you is breaking my heart
When I get out we'll make a fresh start

I know you think I'm lying Whitley
You think I'm going on
I used to think I'm a bad man
Well that bad man has gone

I can't believe I'm sat here Whitley
Sat here without you
But the thought of you out there waiting for me
Is the thought that's getting me through

Things were going great Whitley
Until I came to jail
I love you so much
I cry when I read your mail.
I know you love me too Whitley

And I know that you're the one

But please believe me when I say

You don't know what you've got till it's gone.

Michael

Organizing a poetry competition wherever you work and inviting entries on a theme is something that will be sure to get some people thinking and writing. Of course giving out prizes to offenders can be contentious and I had some difficulty getting a small amount of phone credit to Michael. Almost all the unsolicited poetry I receive from young prisoners is to or about girlfriends and mothers, invariably expressing regret, or it is about bereavement: seemingly more commonplace in prison than it is out here. I'm always meeting lads whose father or brother was murdered or took their own life or whose mother died young; teenagers raised by grandparents from when they started to get into trouble, now back in custody for the umpteenth time and finding those grandparent's lives are ending.

Recently a lad shouted me to his door and pushed something he had written underneath. It was about his mother who had died a few weeks before. He wanted to know if it was any good, wanted my help to write something down about her life, about her addictions, about him and her. I helped him write about his memory of the last normal evening at home, before his mother was herself sent to prison and he was taken into his first institution.

The night is like a normal night except it isn't

I know my mum is in court tomorrow

I imagine my mum will be coming home

She knows she isn't

Excerpt from Dee's memoir work

That is partly what a writer in residence in prison is for: to help prisoners cope with distress, with life inside, by helping them write things down. My experience has been that when a lad is writing about something of great emotional significance to himself, then he is more prepared to search for the right words. When Dee had finished writing his piece about his mother, he stabbed down his last full stop, dropped the pen on the paper *thanks for that boss* and was out the door with the text behind him.

Lads frequently give me assorted pages, whole exercise books of writing about their lives that they don't want back and don't want published. They have written down what happened to them and now they are rid of it. I am aware of a therapeutic writing technique where participants are asked to write about the cause of their pain and then seal it in an envelope. I'm a walking envelope. Writing about emotionally raw experiences can reduce self-harm and even violence to others, and the authors it seems mostly look to poetry as a means of release.

In *Chapter Two* of this book which includes information about autobiographical writing there are a number of exercises using the senses that have served as a basis for poetry, some of which is included therein. Some notes by Dominic about his late father eventually became the poem below.

The Last Goodbye

I remember the taste of slimy whelks
my Granny's caravan at Coney Island,
my hand piercing through the little
milk bottle tops as I picked it out of its shell,
my father's hand turning silver trout in the frying pan.
We would go for walks
carrying me on his shoulders
my hands around his warm forehead.

I remember smoke and beer
the front room a cloud of smoke surrounding him
the tips of his fingers brownish yellowish.
I sanded a board of wood once
brought it home to show him.

I remember sitting across from the sombre priest.

His voice was quiet, a low hush, serious, concerned.

I knew the news was coming but when it did

the un-realness, the loneliness, the shock.

Dominic

I recall how much Dominic enjoyed excavating the memory of his father in the caravan at Coney Island. Memories are the bane of many people I work with. They are phantoms that have been submerged along with the host's receptivity, by drugs and by alcohol and by the compulsion to toughen-up.

Prominent in the images Dominic described were his father's hands. Yet he misses an opportunity in the last stanza to close in on the priest's hands or his own. It was because, he said, he couldn't remember and neither was he prepared to fictionalise for the sake of the poem. Fictionalising elements of significant memories is sometimes a requirement of writing about them and to be encouraged. Paradoxically it can be a way of discovering a truth about an experience. If Dominic had written about the priest's hands touching his, whether it happened or not, it could have been used to contrast with the last time he had touched his father's hands.

Exercise 65   **The Thing You Can't Remember**

Suggest to the participant(s) that they write a poem about a significant event in their life.

- Ask them to focus on a few moments and write down what they remember visually, aurally, kinaesthetically.

- Now ask them to identify something they can't quite recall, an image, what someone said, what the weather was like that day.

- Ask the participant(s) to begin the poem with a description of the thing they can't remember.

Poetry is about experimenting with language as well as our past. Poets alter the meaning of words in pursuit of enhancing our perception of the world. In doing so they can ask a lot of readers, there can be a lot of decoding required, something that most people, never mind the client group of this book, are reluctant to do. One should be careful though, about one's assumptions. I have had a young Jamaican prisoner ask me if he could read W H Auden's villanelle 'If I Could Tell You' to an audience in the chapel, and found many other individuals in the jail with whom I've read and discussed poems I love, like Carol Ann Duffy's 'Warming Her Pearls'.

The poet Pat Winslow introduced me to a writing exercise that opens a door to poetic language and thinking; often best used when one is working with small groups.

Exercise 66	**Nouns and Verbs**

(By kind permission of Pat Winslow)

This exercise requires at least two participants and as the worker you can include yourself.

- Fold a piece of paper down the centre and turn it so that the fold is to your right hand side. Consider the thing you want to write about in terms of nouns.
- Write a list of eight nouns preceded by *the* down the side towards the fold. *The caravan, the priest*…

Turn the paper over so that the fold is to the left and swap with someone else.

- Don't look at the nouns they have written.
- Now write a list of verbs. Ask the participant(s) to search for words they don't normally use.

Unfold the paper and see if any of the nouns are animated by unusual verbs.

The Clock is Always Ticking

My white washed walls
The dusty orange air
The morning shouts
The officers laugh
The wing screams

Prison is no life at all
Minute by minute day by day
I might have years but it's alright
The gates cry the keys deny
Tomorrow will come but go so quickly

Eddie

Half Awake

The windows are calling out
For someone that they know
The barbed wire moans
The rattling keys run across the bars
And enjoy the lock of the door
Whispers in the distance

Clammy air has crept into my cell
And stuck to my window
The itchy covers shed their skin like a snake
Leaving purple polka dots
On my skin
My dreams are always about fighting
But I never win
There are no fences in my sleep

Jamie and Liam

A variation on the nouns and verbs exercise is to apply it to more than one voice in the same poem.

Letter to Natalie

Another night and another day
The exercise yard is lazy and peaceful
My television hammers my brain cells
Medication touches my bloodstream
Soon I'll be dancing out the gates back to you

> *Your freedom threatens me*
> *My fear is you have a key to here*
> *You moan down the phone*
> *My sleeping tablets are scared they'll*
> *All be eaten.*

Can't wait to make it up to you

Daniel

The animation of ordinary nouns is part of everyday speech; the objective here has to be to push the boundaries into the poetic. It was a way of Daniel both recognising and articulating how different his girlfriend might see things. Of course the nouns and verbs exercise can easily be altered to nouns and adjectives.

Exercise 67   **Odd Descriptions**

Ask the participant(s) to write a list of relevant nouns down one side of a page. Do the same yourself. Fold the pages down the centre and swap.

- Don't look at what the other person has written.
- Each of you write a list of adjectives. As a prompt you might suggest the adjectives derive from various headings: mood; size; colour and shade; weight; texture, etc.
- Now pair the nouns and adjectives together. Try and make the marriage unusual, surprising.

I did the exercise with nouns from the piece above and came up with: *sweet tablets; cloudy freedom; tiny yard; acrid day; happy medication.*

In *Chapter Two* on autobiographical writing there are a number of *body-self exercises* where I've suggested we ask people to enter into a dialogue with a problem. When lads have written poetry for me I've suggested they find a way of animating the thing, the issue that is preoccupying them.

The Statue of Regret

The statue of my regret is made of ice
Every good deed melts a slice
Every new morning it returns to life
What can be done to make it right?
I unlocked the door to an ice age
It's a blizzary I've made
My head bowed in a hailstorm of shame
Every good deed done in vain

Chris

Beef

Beef is an uncertain weather forecast
it could be a nice sunny day, then
all of a sudden, it could be thunder.
Beef is an animal, it hunts you
but you also hunt it
until you find it and it finds you.
Beef started over something daft.
Beef is like a disease
beef is like the air
it always hangs around.
Beef can be good
like an adrenalin rush.

Beef once shot at me.
I was seventeen, talking about football
sitting on a wall, with my mates.

Beef is sometimes bright and sometimes dark
never a colour that calms you
the soft blue of water in a pool.

Jason

Exercise 68	**Animal Vegetable Mineral**

Discuss the matter that the participant(s) have in their life.

Define it as an abstraction: *addiction, poverty, jealousy…*

Of course it can also be a positive force: *hope, love, faith…*

Discuss its qualities: if it were a colour, a sound, a texture, a taste, a creature, a plant.

Ask the participant(s) to write a poem that tells us: how it was born or made, what does it live upon, what it needs to survive and how it can be destroyed.

To support such exercises I'll use a colour chart commandeered from somewhere such as B&Q, and when I was working in a YOT I had a touch box of varying textures to serve as a stimulus for exercises.

Hearing the echo of the cell
When there's just me in it
Surrounded by green oxide walls
The colour of nothing done
And the drone of the fan

Jason (aged 15 on Supervision)

Touch box and colour charts: writing exercise in a youth club

I used the box by firstly discussing significant memories with the young people, asking them to reach into the touch box to discover something that reminded them of the experience. They then had to describe the sensation and how it related to the memory (they were not allowed to look at the material). Then I'd ask them to think of a second significant memory but not to tell me what it is, rather to reach into the box and describe a related sensation. I would then hazard a guess at the nature of the memory.

I've benefited from a number of Poetry School[1] courses over the last few years and have naturally borrowed and adapted exercises from the workshops to use myself. The following two I gleaned from workshops run by poet Alicia Stubbersfield,[2] and I've included them here with her kind permission.

1. The Poetry School, 81 Lambeth Walk, London SE11 6DX (020 7582 1679) http://www. poetryschool.com/index.php
2. Alicia Stubbersfield. Tutor in creative writing at Liverpool John Moores University. Her publications include: *The Magician's Assistant* (1994), Newcastle: Flambard Press; *Unsuitable Shoes* (1999), Gwent: The Collective Press; and *Joking Apart* (2006), Gwent: The Collective Press.

Exercise 69   **Do the Opposite**

Ask the participant(s) to select a theme for a poem: love, hope, honesty, revenge, forgiveness, etc.

Ask them to think of half a dozen images, places, sounds, etc. that they associate with that theme.

For love for example, it might (or might not be) be a river, for hope, a sunny morning.

Now ask them to write down the opposite of each. For example, the opposite of a sunny morning might be, a wintry night, of the river a desert.

Ask the participant(s) to work the opposites into their poems.

When we write about significant events and transitions that others can relate to, there's a risk of the over familiar too predictable, simile or image. Considering opposites can be a means of finding something fresh and effective.

Anger

A flash of red and my chest goes tight
Knot in the stomach ready to fight
Hail is beating down all around
Eagle calls out a deafening sound
Wonder if my feet even touch the ground

Now I lay in my bed
Can barely remember that vibrant red
Close my eyes into the blue skies
Warm soft rain stroking my skin

The eagle's gone blue tit's asking where I've been

A sigh of relief and comfort consumes me

Cruising through blue

Never again

Anon

Exercise 70 **No Fairytale**

Ask the participant(s) to

- tell you about their favourite fairytales (see *Telling Tales* exercise in *Chapter 4*)

- to think of an everyday action; and

- a question about their life.

Then work all three into the same poem.

Glynn and a Big Peach

Off to the local shop

I need a quick pick me up

Fags won't do it neither will beer

I need a few peaches and I know they're near

I've had to get out of the gaff

Our marriage has become a bit of laugh

I go to the pub she soaks in the bath

Carry on like this it'll be a thing of the past

I've tried to show her all I can

I'm thinking now maybe I ain't the man

She wants more than I can give

She's lost interest in the gig

I wish this peach would carry me

Up in the sky far from Accrington

Life isn't a fairytale that won't happen

I could scoff the lot

And go back to square one

Or save one for her

And see how we get on

Glynn

The second exercise offers us the opportunity to make unexpected and fanciful connections, to seek parallels that are not obvious.

The biggest factor that both drives and hinders expression in lad's writing at the YOI (as with the above) is rhyme. This is the case for two reasons. It is a commonly held belief that all poetry has to rhyme; if it doesn't rhyme what else is there to make it a poem? The second is the ubiquitous presence of rap within the jail and in the wider cultural life of the prisoners.

I've worked hard to steer lads away from rhyme. I began by suggesting that poems need not rhyme, and then progressed to refusing to allow rhyme and eventually insisting that lads unrhymed their work. I took stock when hardened offenders apologised to me for the odd couplet. As much as I've tried to evade the rap and lyrics genre, it has pursued me and induced me to collaborate. When Barack Obama was elected President of the United States a lad who was well-known in the prison as a rapper saw his opportunity and asked me to help him write a celebratory poem, which I insisted mustn't rhyme. My terms made the exercise pointless to him and he wore me down, firstly by his incessant rhyming, then his increasingly rhythmic reading, until by the time of his performance in the library I was introducing him into a microphone over a pre-recorded hip hop beat.

Black Man in the White House

Barack's been elected

Bush has been ejected

From the thing called the White House

It'll soon turn black when Bush turns the lights out

Barack painted the town like a night out

Brought tears to my eyes I nearly cried out

He got votes from Alabama right up to Montana

They called him a Muslim

Just cos he's black

Sly digs to attack Barack

He didn't back down

Bounced right back

Took it on the chin kept his pride intact

Now's America's on track

There's rumours they wanna shoot Barack

Before they do that he better pull troops out of Iraq

He's an inspiration to the younger generation

He's got a way with words — could he be my relation?

Only difference is he's leading a nation

I'm busting rhymes we both need some patience

He lives by his oratory giving him authority

So remember remember the fourth of November

McCain's got the boot Barack's the contender

It's yes we can from Jan to December

No matter what race

No matter what gender

Callum

There's no doubt that rap aspires towards linguistic agility and not all of it is written from and about the wrong side of the tracks, from under a self-aggrandising cloak of malice.

It's also the case that we should respond to those who are experimenting with the written and spoken word; we should work with what they are already doing, but with a view to introducing them to something new. Generally rap doesn't foster reading, nor writing much either, it's an oral form often egotistical in content and harsh in style with a need to denigrate rather than celebrate. Occasionally it can redeem itself for me through alliteration and humour, but generally it's the predictable aggressive posturing that I dislike. It is the sound of our times and socially we are not living in a progressive era.

The tendency in arts work with offenders, particularly young offenders, to shy away from a challenge needs to be resisted more. Too often interventions merely take what is already being said and present it back to the participants in a form they are familiar with. Everyone feels validated but nobody is left curious. Arts interventions should leave participants feeling that they are lacking something. They should give people an appetite and some idea of how it can be sated.

6.1   Poem from a Poem

A good starting point to ask someone to write a poem can be another poem. Something that they like or something you suggest. It's a way of deciding upon a theme or a style that is accessible to the writer. There are a number of poems I use for this, one is 'This Moment' by Evan Boland.[3] It is a sparse, short, evocative poem describing, as the opening two lines tell us, a neighbourhood, at dusk. The reader you feel is standing at the edge of the scene, just out of sight, observing houses and nature. At the end of the poem a mother is reunited with her child and a door closes. The poem has a haunting, yet light touch. I ask lads to write about a street of their own at dusk, and to describe a house. To try and conjure up an atmosphere the way Evan Boland has about somewhere they know intimately in as few words and lines as possible.

---

3. 'This Moment' from *In a Time of Violence* (1994), W W Eavan Boland, New York: Norton & Company, Inc.

Original version
of Friday by Dan

'Curriculum Vitae'[4] is a poem by Lisel Mueller that works very well as an impulse for autobiographical poetry and it continues to be a fruitful resource for me. Lisel Mueller was born in Hamburg in 1924. The poem is a series of 20 sequential short stanzas that move through her life markers in unadorned and penetrating language. She describes her childhood and family life in Germany, the rise of Fascism, emigration, marriage, her own children and ageing, one or two sentences at a time. Lads rarely get beyond point ten, but then I'm generally working with people who haven't reached 21. It's an exercise in brevity and encourages the writer to decide on salient images and events that epitomise their past.

---

4. 'Curriculum Vitae' from *Alive Together: New and Selected Poems* (1996), Lisel Mueller, Baton Rouge, Los Angeles: Louisiana State University Press.

1 I was born in a Lancashire town
   Its name means the black lake

2 I remember drinking the last of the milk
   Being chased through the hallway laughing my head off
   The nights were good, wild cats, hot custard and warm chats
   The cat's eyes were glowing in the dark.

3 Behind my cottage wild bushes grew, pond and spring
   Spring water splashing the pond's silver surface

4 My demeanour struck down
   Whipped and lashed into depression

5 I sought happiness through cannabis. Wide smile glazed eyes
   Paranoia wrapped around my neck like a noose

6 I got caught sleeping in my school at night
   Locked out by my own father
   When I was arrested my father said
   Take him away—"Son of mine no more!"
   Could you do that?

7 He came round to drive a car through the door
   And I never saw him again
   Not a pair of shoes in ten years

8 I did some things. Some things you wouldn't like me for
   I tick off weeks like days
   Try to get on well with the officers

Jamie

My favourite line is *Not a pair of shoes in ten years*. Initially it was something he said in answer to a question and I told him to write it down. It sounded so beyond his years, very Lancashire and a remark that can only refer to a parent.

My demeanour struk down
whipped and lashed into depression.
I seeked happiness through canabis, wide smile, glazed eyes
paranoa wrapped around my neck like A Noose

Original draft CV by Jamie.

1   I was born at the end of the largest cul–de–sac in England. In front of the towering cranes. Behind me a horizon of hills.

2   I was born when blood was given for oil.

3   My parents were wild. They were people locked together. A swan and a goose in a cage, one meal between them.

4   At my grandma's I found a space and place to be my childish self…

Chris

Other poems I have used in this context are: 'Felicity in Turin' by Paul Durcan, 'Scorpion' by Jo Shaopcott, 'Mid Term Break' by Seamus Heaney, 'The Horses' by Pablo Neruda, 'Love in a Bathtub' by Sujata Bhatt, 'Temptation' by Nina Cassian.

6.2   Personal and Public Events

Exercise 71   I Read the News Today

Ask the participant(s) to write a poem about a significant personal event in their own life: a birth, death, marriage, love affair or break up, or conversely something achieved.

Ask them to include in the poem a reference from the news regarding someone else's experience.

She died the same week as Princess Diana.
I remember waiting for her to come home, even after I knew.
Elton John played at my mother's funeral too.

Lawrence

I remember planes going into buildings
people running from danger
sirens and firemen
hysterical commentators in America.
We watched this in silence.
We buried my uncle the day before.

Anon

The comparison can give the personal experience more impact. The author of the second extract, who is a British Muslim, told me the family felt guilty about the grief they felt for the death of his uncle in the context of 9/11, but it is felt nonetheless.

Autobiographical poetry can be described as an effort to give a shape to the things that shaped us to begin with, and there are many doors we can lead people to, to locate the influences (the second exercise is again courtesy of Alicia Stubbersfield who told me she picked it up from poet Michael Laskey).

Exercise 72   **Influences**

Ask the participant(s) to think of something that they've kept even though they no longer have a use for it. It might be an old item of clothing.

* Why have they kept it?
* What memories are connected to it?
* Ask them to write a poem about the object.

Ask the participant(s) to write down something a member of their family once said to them — then to consider their reaction at the time, and how they see the remark now.

* Ask them to write a poem that includes that remark.

Give the participant(s) an arbitrary opening line for their poem. For example: *The first thing I packed was…; Only now I realise…; I waited until…; As soon as I found out…etc.* The poem they write must be autobiographical.

Present the participant(s) with a box or a container of any kind.

* Ask them what's in it. Their poem must begin: *In the box…* and it must be autobiographical.

Discussion Suggestion 24

How have other people influenced who you are?

How much of who you are is down to you?

What influence have you had on other people's lives?

Ultimately poetry is not just about self-expression but also about the making of it. For me, poems that tell all on a first reading are the least satisfying, I want something I have to return to and fathom out. For most lads at the jail poetry is of comfort and pleasure, it is not a craft of interest. It is usually the first form that people will reach for, and partly because there are 500 prisoners and one part-time writer, I look for the lads who will read and re-read, draft and redraft for its own sake. The other reason of course is that the lads who are least likely to come back through the gate are the lads who are prepared to persevere against the odds.

ACTION INTO WORDS

7

Far-reaching public spending cuts, represented in the criminal justice system as a 'rehabilitation revolution' and 'payment by results',
will almost certainly mean that there is less opportunity for con-
centrated individual and small group work with offenders.[1] In the
Arts Council spending round of 2011 the Writers in Prison Network
(WPN) received an award of nil funding. The range of the WPN's
achievements is far beyond the work set out in this book. It has
included film-making, storytelling and song-writing at institutions
that include secure accommodation for children to high security
prisons and even a British Army correctional facility. Many widely
published and produced writers have passed through its ranks, yet
there is currently a fight for its continued existence. Then again it
is not going to be easy for any government to wane in the struggle
against criminal behaviour; not in the UK, not in England. International trend surveys show that the British public is more concerned
with crime and violence than people from other European countries
and even the US.

Britain continues to have the highest imprisonment rate in Europe
and law and order is frequently identified as the most important
issue facing the country today. Surveys also show that the public at
large have little faith in authority's ability to apprehend and reform
criminals in general.[2] The empirical evidence continues to demand
more money, more time and effort not less; and this before the riots
of August 2011.

---

1. Bird, H and Albertson (nee Wilkinson) K E (2011) 'Prisoners as Citizens, Big Society and
   the Rehabilitation Revolution: Truly Revolutionary?' *British Journal of Community Justice*,
   Vol. 9 (1/2): 93–109.
2. http://www.ipsos-mori.com/researchpublications/researcharchive/314/Britons-Most-
   Worried-By-Crime-8212-And-Government-Is-Least-Trusted-To-Deal-With-It.aspx

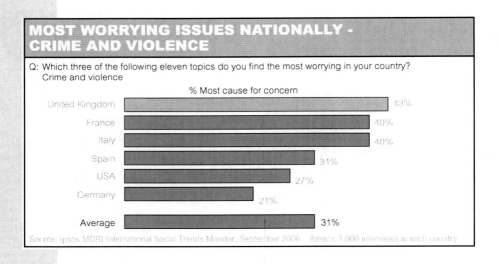

MOST WORRYING ISSUES NATIONALLY - CRIME AND VIOLENCE

Q: Which three of the following eleven topics do you find the most worrying in your country? Crime and violence

% Most cause for concern

United Kingdom	43%
France	40%
Italy	40%
Spain	31%
USA	27%
Germany	21%
Average	31%

Source: Ipsos MORI International Social Trends Monitor, September 2006   Base: c.1,000 interviews in each country

Those riots were so unprecedented in their proliferation, violence, and, in places, vicious materialism that they not only force an interrogation of our society's values but question its worth in certain locations. No one at the prison seemed the slightest bit surprised or perturbed by the events of August 2011. Officers and lads are fairly unshockable. Working or living in a jail you acquire a sense of an ever increasing volume of young men habituated to crime, schooled in a dog eat dog Britain.

Sentencing of perpetrators so far has had people referred to the Crown Court for imprisonment on charges that in other circumstances would have merited a short community penalty, even a caution. A great many of those arrested were arbitrarily and inappropriately remanded into custody; a draconian precedent that left officers with an influx of vulnerable prisoners. The prison population, NOMS and YOT caseloads are spiking. I am beginning to sit down with lads involved in the national public disorder, asking them to write about what they have done, in the first person and the third, or through the eyes of a shopkeeper; getting them to spell out the motives behind their actions, the cost of the things they have stolen against the intangible damage done.

He felt he had to go. He knew his friends would be there. Walking up the road we noticed most normal people hurrying home. We could tell it was a dangerous night. Squads of blacked out youths, rarely seen, rushed into town. People looked like they were following orders. Young people on bikes, geared up for war in black bandanas and crime gear. Soldiers missing guns. Some were even older, the leaders, the generals looked like they'd never grown up. Although nervous we eventually fell in with them. It was just us and the troops. "Which way?" "Whichever way they go" he replied but looking surprised at himself. Closer to the town centre we were forced to make a choice. Alleys and main streets were cordoned off by the police, dressed in black and clearly ready for action. The elite guard of town with their shiny shields were terrifying and made their point well. "We better turn around" I suggested. But he was not to be deterred....

Syd

Lads in the prison via the riots are reportedly less at ease in the environment than most, better educated and easier to work with.[3] A few were students and it seems obvious that they would never have seen the inside of a jail were it not for being involved in that event. One or two have told me that they initially saw the riots as a form of anarchic protest and went along out of fascination, to take photos or otherwise support some kind of inchoate rebellion.

There were people there that you never normally see in town, people that think they don't belong there.

But then events unfolded to the sobering spectacle of looters attacking other looters to steal recently stolen property as 'girls were dragged down alleys by groups of men'. The impression I've drawn is that young men were just shopping through shop windows and any references to a banker's bonus or educational maintenance allowance is in the mind of newspaper columnists and not in the lad in

---

3. See writing exercise on English riots in *Appendix 1.*.

front of me. My sense is that this could have happened under any government and has been a long time in the making.

I can see how undertaking writing with rioters would provoke the ire of people in a way it wouldn't with a car thief, but it enables us to challenge people individually who have been sentenced collectively and despite the climate we should not be defensive about this kind of work or arts work in general. Contrary to assumptions many arts organizations do seem to make a point of evidencing the effectiveness of what they do and the Arts Alliance has compiled an extensive evidence library.[4]

In 2010 the Writers in Prison Network commissioned Sheffield Hallam University's Centre for Community Justice to conduct a year-long evaluation of its work. This has involved weekly journals, observations, interviews with prisoners and before and after appraisals. The final report is due in 2012. For my part, prisoners at the YOI tell me that they find it useful, that it makes them think about why they are there.

People who never dreamed of writing put pen to paper because they are being asked to explain themselves and give vent to their demons. I know that for some of them it may already be too late; that some of them want to work with me to get out of cleaning the wing, their pad or what passes for education, but if one could rely on the testimonies of prisoners alone the network would have no difficulty in securing funding.

> Since I came to prison I started working with Mr Crowley. I am in prison for burglary and Mr Crowley asked me if I wanted to do a poem for three voices which I was more than happy to do. I never had feelings for any of my victims because I didn't understand what I was doing. Since working with Mr Crowley I have thought long and hard about what I have done and how my victims feel and I have learned a lot. I think what Mr Crowley is doing is very good and a lot of people benefit from it and it will help people who are afraid to attend education. I also told my probation officer what I have been doing with Mr

---

4. *Arts Alliance Evidence Library* (PDF) Angus McLewin Associates March 2011. http://www.clinks.org/assets/files/PDFs/Arts%20Alliance/Arts_Evidence_Library.pdf

Crowley and he was pleased with me and said there had been a change in me. I think the course is very good and I am thankful for what Mr Crowley has done with me.

Liam

The consequences of poor literacy levels for individuals and for our society are serious and arguably farther reaching than many people realise. The National Literacy Trust report *Literacy Changes Lives*[5] includes data that shows how poor literacy is prominent across disadvantaged adult lives. The presence of poor literacy may or may not reflect direct causal connections in employment, poor health, family life, civic and cultural engagement etc., but…

> …low literacy levels are a barrier to social justice. They produce social, economic and cultural exclusion that scars communities and undermines social cohesion….the literacy agenda sits at the heart of the desire to improve personal wellbeing, create safer and stronger communities… [6]

Unlike other interventions writing can be a means to address not only literacy but therapeutic needs, moral reasoning, offence-focused thinking and all at the same time. My experience of the criminal justice system tells me that much more work has to be done with the written word. In all the YOIs, adult jails and secure training centres I visit, it is telling how many screens I see in proportion to books and writing paper, in cells, on wings, and in classrooms.

Computers in the classroom is supposedly the universal emblem of investment, but what is really needed is people sitting down with pen and paper, slowly writing their thoughts out, reading aloud to others, correcting and improving, then typing up the tangible when it's finally done. Creative writing as a means to address offending, far from being at threat, should be built upon, not just by the Arts

---

5.   Dugdale G and Clark C (2008), *Literacy Changes Lives: An Advocacy Resource*, London: National Literacy Trust.
6.   *Ibid*, Foreword.

Council, but by NOMS, the Prison Service, YOTs, education providers, even employers; after all its work is of value to everyone in society.

Using writing effectively with offenders is a specialist role and whilst it is easier to train writers about criminal justice there are I know many teachers, librarians, prison officers, NOMS and YOT workers who are already helping people to reflect and learn through writing and who would welcome training and support. Effective arts work needs longevity and consistency. The ineffective arts work is often a product of people being parachuted in for a few days, who in their defence have little opportunity to get to know the people they are trying to engage.

I know my work and that of other writers has played its part in resettlement and restorative justice, but I suspect writers in prisons in general could be more integrated into reducing re-offending strategies. There is an argument for prison writers to be used more to support discipline by being a service that's only available to prisoners whose behaviour is positive (in the context of the environment) or at least not defiant to the regime. For example, I won't work with lads who have been sent to the block (segregation) because their behaviour has resulted in loss of privileges.

As well as the financial threat that this kind of work faces, there is an educational or ideological risk to it as well. Education everywhere in Britain these days, it seems, has to be vocationally justified, and this is especially the case in prisons, on the face of it a logical position. But there is little point putting prisoners through industrial cleaning courses if they believe it is morally acceptable to employ violence or sell drugs to get an income.

Some lads undertaking the pre-release course at my YOI are quite candid that they do not need help with CVs or with signing on, because leaving custody they will be going back to 'grafting'. That is their career. Perhaps they are in a minority overall but there is something more profound than employability that needs to be tackled.

Interventions rarely succeed in isolation; rehabilitation practitioners work in a context of reflective practice and require a comprehensive range of interventions at their disposal to use with many different individuals.

My hope is that the exercises here will be beneficial to existing preventative work, at routine NOMS and YOT appointments, as well as in more structured programmes in and out of custody. Possibly it is the basis of a distinct programme itself.

APPENDIX 1

SOME SUGGESTED WRITING EXERCISE MODELS

A.1 To use in victim awareness work

Exercise 73   **Victim Awareness: Session One**

Revisit the offence with the offender in detail. Initially employ automatic writing exercises (*Chapter Two*). Some nouns down the margin should be arbitrary to get the participant(s) into the feel of the exercise. Some should be connected to the offence, some to the senses;

Ask the participant(s) to write a first person, present tense monologue set during the commission of the offence that employs all the senses. Ask them to slow the offence down, what are they doing and feeling at every stage?

Discussion Suggestion 25

Are there episodes of the offence they'd sooner forget?

Which aspects of the offence do they find most hard to talk or write about?

Why?

Exercise 74	**Victim Awareness: Session Two**

Repeat both of the above from the victim's perspective.

Then ask the participant(s) to write about the offence in the past tense. How do they see it now?

Discussion Suggestion 26

If they see the offence differently now, what has changed in them?

If they don't, what hasn't?

Exercise 75	**Victim Awareness: Session Three**

If the offence was a burglary/criminal damage/ theft and the victim was not present, get the participant(s) to write some dialogue between themselves and the victim during the commission of the offence (see *Hologram Dialogue* in *Chapter Five*).

The participant(s) have to justify what they are doing as well as see it from the point of view of the victim. If they can't, what does that tell us?

Exercise 76   **Victim Awareness: Session Four**

Ask the participant(s) to think of someone who is close to them.

Then ask them to think of something that belongs to that person, something of value, prefer-ably sentimental and imagine that it has been stolen.

Ask the participant(s) to choose ten letters from the alphabet at random. They should then use the letters to begin words that express how they feel about what has happened. I.e. *Keeps me awake at night, Like to get my hands on them, Police should do more…*

The participant(s) are about to meet the perpetrator.

They have to write a monologue describing calmly how they feel about what has happened.

Discussion Suggestion 27

What would be a just outcome in the above situation?

What is the difference between justice and revenge?

| Exercise 77 | **Victim Awareness: Session Five** |

Ask the participant(s) to describe an incident when they were victimised.

- Perhaps they were robbed or the family home was burgled.
- The key thing is that they were emotionally and/or psychologically affected by the experience.

Ask them to write a letter to the perpetrator of the offence or the injustice.

You may want to employ an automatic writing exercise, employing senses and emotions.

Now ask the participant(s) to write a letter to a victim of an offence which they have committed, explaining their actions.

Discussion Suggestion 28

How can we tell when people are being sincere; when we are face to face with them; when they write to us?

Do apologies and explanations help?

How and why?

A.2 Working with someone who has a drug or alcohol problem

Ask the participant(s) to write a description (from an outsider's point of view in the third person) of the drunken or drug-induced self. We are looking for a physical, verbal and psychological description.

Ask the participant(s) to write a short monologue (100-200 words) justifying their drinking or drug use to a member of their family. (See *Chapter Five* for *Monologues*)

Ask the participant(s) to enter into dialogue with the craving. (See the *Me Myself I* exercise *Chapter Two*). The craving has to try and entice a participant into partaking.

Take the participant(s) through the *Nouns and Verbs* exercise regarding their drug and alcohol problem. (See *Chapter Six*). Nouns should apply to drug and alcohol use. Make the verbs as uncommon as you can.

Exercise 78   **Animating the Abstract**

Ask the participant(s) to think of their addiction and/or the craving in other forms.

If my craving were a musical instrument it would be…

If my addiction were a piece of music it would sound like…

Continue using an animal…the weather…a plant…a place real or mythical.

See also the *Animal Mineral Vegetable* exercise in *Chapter Six*.

A.3 Working with someone who needs to address something in their past

Ask the participant(s) to take part in *Today My Hand* and *Once My Hand* exercises (see *Chapter Two*). The *Once My Hand* exercise should refer to the event in the past.

Use the appropriate *Automatic Writing* exercise from *Chapter Two* to help get a fuller description of the event.

Use the two *Witness Statement* exercises in *Chapter Two* then…

Exercise 79   **Once it Did This to Me**

Ask the participant(s) to think of a relationship that was affected by the event from the past.

Ask them to think of a specific scene in the relationship where the event got in the way.

Get or help the participant(s) to write the scene — in the past tense and the third person, I.e. this was something that happened to someone else in the past.

A.4   Working with someone who needs to address anger and aggression

Exercise 80   **Anger Storms In**

Ask the participant(s) to think of the first time in their lives they can recall being angry and acting aggressively.

Ask them to write about the incident in the third person, the omniscient point of view.

How did their behaviour seem from the outside?

Describe it physically and aurally.

Was their behaviour justified?

What was the outcome and the effect on others?

Ask them to think of the last time they acted aggressively.

Again describe the behaviour in the third person but from the point of view of the person on the receiving end.

Exercise 81	**Anger Storms Out**

Ask the participant(s) to recall a situation where they got angry.

Ask them to think of anger as an external voice, a character.

Get them to create the character as someone else. (see *Chapter Three* for creating characters)

Now ask them to write a page of dialogue between themselves (Mr or Ms Calm) and Mr or Ms Anger set in the situation.

Anger gets progressively angrier trying to rile them into action; into aggression but doesn't succeed.

Discussion Suggestion 29

Ask the participant (s): do you think self talk might help in situations where you feel yourself getting progressively angry?

Suggest that they remove themselves from the argument next time and try it.

A.5 Exploring Empathy in General

Many of the exercises will test empathetic ability but it is particularly worth looking at the character creation exercises *Someone Like You*, *The Good and Bad in Everyone* and the dialogue exercise in *Chapter Five, Power and its Uses*.

Exercise 82	A Riot of My Own

Ask participant(s) who were involved in the English riots of 2011 to:

- describe their own actions as if they a bystander or a friend who didn't want to be involved;
- write a monologue in the voice of a shopkeeper or shop worker the morning after their shop is looted;
- the afternoon before.

Discussion Suggestion 30

If more people around you are committing offences, does it make it more acceptable for you to?

Can only those who have never committed a crime condemn those who have?

APPENDIX 2
FURTHER READING

A.1 Select Bibliography

Armitage, Simon, *Kid*. London: Faber & Faber (1992)

Ayckbourn, Alan, *The Crafty Art of Playmaking*. London: Faber & Faber (2002)

Baikie K and Wilhelm K, 'Emotional and Physical Health Benefits of Expressive Writing', *Advances in Psychiatric Treatment*. (2005) Volume 11:338-346. www.apt.rcpsych.org

Baim, Brookes, Mountford, *The Geese Theatre Handbook*. Hook: Waterside Press (1992)

Bloom, Harold, *Shakespeare (The Invention of the Human)*. London: Fourth Estate (1998)

Boal, Augusto, *Games for Actors and Non-Actors*. London: Routledge. (1992)

Campbell, Joseph, *The Hero with a Thousand Faces*. London: Fontana Press (1948)

Clark, Christina and Dugdale, George, 'The Role of Literacy in Offender Behaviour' (Nov 2008) *Literacy Changes Lives Series*. National Literacy Trust www.literacytrust.org.uk

Cox, Murray and Theilgaard, Alice, *Shakespeare as Prompter: Amending Imagination and the Therapeutic Process*. London: Jessica Kingsley (1994)

Cullen, Murray and Freeman-Longo, Robert E, *Men and Anger*. Holyoke, MA, USA NEARI Press (1996)

Egri, Lajos, *The Art of Dramatic Writing*. London: Simon & Schuster (1946)

Fountain, Tim, *So You Want to Be A Playwright?* London: Nick Hern Books (2007)

Greig, Noel, *Playwriting (A Practical Guide)*. Routledge: London (2005)

Hoggart, Richard, *The Way We Live Now.* London: Pimlico (1995)

James, Oliver, *Affluenza.* London: Vermillion (2007)

James, Oliver, *Juvenile Violence in a Winner-loser Culture: Socio-economic and Familial Origins of the Rise of Violence Against the Person.* London: Free Association Books (1995)

Leland, Christopher, *The Art of Compelling Fiction,* Cincinnati, Ohio, USA: Story Press (1998)

McKee, Robert, *Story; Substance, Structure, Style and the Principles of Screenwriting.* London: Methuen (1999)

Salzman, Mark, *True Notebooks.* London: Bloomsbury (2004)

Wertenbaker, Timberlake, *Our Country's Good.* London: Methuen (1990)

A.2   Further Reading

Armitstead, Julian, *After the Accident.* London: Methuen Drama (2011)

Blom-Cooper Sir Louis, *The Penalty of Imprisonment.* London and New York: Continuum (2008)

Crowley, Michael, *The Man They Couldn't Hang,* Hook: Waterside Press (2010)

James, Erwin, *A Life Inside.* London: Guardian Books (2003)

Liebling, Alison and Price, David, *The Prison Officer.* Hook: Waterside Press (2001)

McGuire, James, *Understanding Psychology and Crime,* Milton Keynes: Open University Press (2004)

A.3   Some Organizations and Periodicals

▢ Arts Alliance
artsalliance.ning.com
A national body for the promotion of arts in the Criminal Justice Sector.

▢ *British Journal of Community Justice*

A peer reviewed journal with three issues per annual volume published jointly by De Montfort University and Sheffield Hallam University.

◻ English PEN
www.englishpen.org
'Defending the rights of persecuted writers to promoting literature in translation and sending writers in to refugee centres and prisons".

◻ The Koestler Trust
www.koestlertrust.org.uk
Arts by Offenders

◻ Lapidus
www.lapidus.org.uk
'Promoting creative writing and reading for health and wellbeing'.

◻ National Literacy Trust
www.literacytrust.org.uk
Campaigns to improve public understanding of the vital importance of literacy.

◻ *Not Shut Up*
www.notshutup.org
Quarterly magazine of prisoner's writing and artwork.

◻ The Poetry School
www.poetryschool.com
81 Lambeth Walk City of London, SE11 6DX (020 7582 1679)

◻ *Prison Service Journal*
Available online and to download at www.hmprisonservice.gov.uk

◻ Road Peace

www.roadpeace.org
A national charity for road crash victims which is an independently funded membership organization. Members include those who have been bereaved or injured in road crashes and also those who are concerned about road danger. It was awarded Charity of the Year by *The Guardian* in 2008.

¤ *Women in Prison*
A magazine sent free to women's prisons. It's also an outlet for women's art and writing. 347 -349 City Road, London EC1V 1LR. Helpline: 0800 9530125

¤ Writers in Prison Network
www.writersinprisonnetwork.org
PO Box 7, Welshpool, SY21 0WB

INDEX

Putting justice into words

Why Did You Do It?

Explanations for Offending by Young Offenders in Their Own Words

by Jackie Worrall

Foreword by Paul McDowell

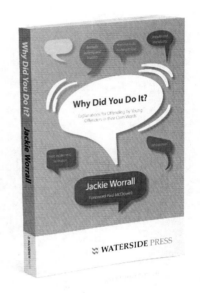

The voices of young offenders—the real life stories behind the worrying and sometimes tragic lives of those who get into trouble with the law. Setting these within the context of descriptions of youth justice policy, Jackie Worrall conveys to her readers an understanding of how and why young people become offenders going far beyond that to be gleaned from everyday rhetoric and theory.

❝ Having worked with offenders for decades, Jackie Worrall's experience and knowledge is unparalleled ❞

Paul McDowell, CEO, Nacro

Paperback ISBN 978-1-904380-74-0 | Ebook ISBN 978-1-906534-08-3

176 pages | January 2012

Full details **WatersidePress.co.uk/WDYDI**

**Available from Prolebooks, Michael Crowley's
debut poetry collection,** *Close to Home*

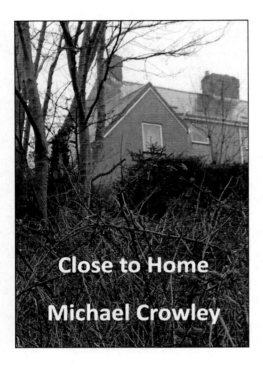

In his debut collection, *Close to Home*, poet and playwright, Michael Crowley, brings together three separate lives to create one existence in a collection that explores a displaced childhood, misplaced adults and the private moments that map a life.

❝ These poems are concerned, in part, with how our environment shapes us, and how we respond to the explicit and implicit rules of those environments. Michael Crowley colours these places by focusing on the people who inhabit them, fills them with the sound of their voices, and packs them with the paraphernalia of habit, obsession and devotion. This pamphlet is an invitation to experience life elsewhere, in another skin ❞

Sarah Hymas

❝ *Close to Home* shows Michael Crowley's ability to conjure place, character and emotion with no sentimentality but taking us right up to that edge so we are moved, delighted or, sometimes, horrified. The poems are lyrical and down-to-earth, urban with an understanding of how nature is a positive force in our lives ❞

Alicia Stubbersfield

Full details **www.prolebooks.co.uk**